Rock Climbing
Western
Oregon

The Rogue

The Contributions of Oregon Climbers
Edited and Illustrated by Greg Orton

Mountain N' Air Books — La Crescenta, CA. 91214

ROCK CLIMBING
WESTERN OREGON, The ROGUE Region

Copyright 2005© by Greg Orton.
All rights reserved. No portion of this book may be reproduced or utilized in any form, or by any electronic, mechanical, or other means without the prior written permission of the author.

Published in the United States of America by:
Mountain N' Air Books
P. O. Box 12540
La Crescenta CA 91224

mountain-n-air.com — (800) 446-9696, fax: (800) 303-5578
e-mail: publishers@mountain-n-air.com

Layout and Graphics by Greg Orton
Front Cover: Jim Anglin, Turret Syndrome (5.10 c/d), Chris Fralick
Cover Page: Dennis Daugherty peering around from HangTen (5.10a, McKinley Rock), Courtesy of Dennis Daugherty.

Table Of Contents: Mandy Bucey (10) climbing Bugoff (5.6, Emigrant Lake). Photo: Greg Orton.

Library of Congress Catalog Card Number: 2005931212

Greg Orton, 1956 —
Rock Climbing Guide, Oregon State

ISBN: 1-879415-46-1
ISBN13:978-1-879415-46-1

This three-volume series replaces the 2001 edition of Rock Climbing Southwest Oregon.

Rock Climbing Western Oregon, Volume 1, WILLAMETTE
Rock Climbing Western Oregon, Volume 2, UMPQUA
Rock Climbing Western Oregon, Volume 3, ROGUE

Rock Climbing
Western
Oregon

WARNING: ROCK CLIMBING CAN BE HAZARDOUS TO YOUR HEALTH.
No guidebook can act as a substitute for careful planning and appropriate training. Know your personal limits; it is incumbent upon any user of this guide to recognize his/her skills, experience, and confidence to assess and mitigate the risks inherent to each climb they attempt. The purpose of this guide is to provide a historic record of rock climbing in Southwest Oregon. It is a compilation of unverified information gathered from many different climbers. The author cannot verify the accuracy of any of the information in this book, including topo and route descriptions, difficulty ratings, and protection ratings. Bolt placements on topo drawings are approximations, and ratings are subjective and prone to error.

PUBLIC RECREATIONAL USE OF PRIVATE LANDS:
It is public policy of the State of Oregon to encourage owners of land to make their land available to the public by limiting their liability *(105.660)*.
Private landowners owe no duty of care to keep the land safe for entry or use by others for recreational purposes, or to give any warning of a dangerous condition, use, structure or activity on the land to persons entering for recreation *(105.665.1)*. Landowners who directly or indirectly invite or permit any person to use the land for any recreational purpose without charge do not thereby: a) extend any assurance that the land is safe; b) confer upon such persons the legal status of an invitee or licensee to whom a duty of care is owed; or c) assume responsibility for incur liability for any injury, death or loss to any person or property causedby an act or omission of that person *(105.665.2)*. *1991* Oregon Revised Status, pursuant to *ORS 171.275*.

"Though you may read, mark, and learn all Alpine Scriptures, their inward digestion is a matter of a lifetime."
—*H. Tydale*

Dedicated to
Issac, Levi, Katie, Molly
and Brooke

In Memory of
Jim Davis

Dedication
Tribute to Jim Davis (1965-2002)

Jim started climbing in the mid eighties and we enjoyed many a road trip to Smith, plus spring breaks spent in Bishop, Red Rocks, other places. Hueco Tanks was classic. He finished his last final exam on Friday, spent the whole night packing (not sleeping of course) and then drove straight through to El Paso! Coffee anybody? We bouldered our fingers bloody, climbed the highest peak in Texas, went to Carlsbad Caverns, White Sands, some cool little limestone crag with great routes, and ate some authentic Mexican food—all in four days. Oh yeah, near the border checkpoint we fixed the front wheel of the Celica. One lug left holding it on as we blew down the highway at 85 or so. Then he dropped by his sister's house for a quick visit on the way home. She lives in Steamboat Springs Colorado.

Jimmy was the night owl who stayed up until three a.m. to fix a binding on his ski for the trip into the backcountry later that day—with a planned start at around five a.m. Of course anyone else would have fixed it the night before in five minutes. Jimmy started at seven or so, but then he got an idea. Up all night again. Always reinventing the wheel. That's one of the things we liked about Jim, always trying to make something better than the engineers who designed it. Engineering was one of his degrees after all, and although his manipulations didn't always work, he came up with a few nifty gadgets. If I had a dime for every engine he put in his Subaru! He was truly talented in many ways. There really was genius to his madness, er, was it the other way around?

Jim was always enthusiastic for all things outdoors. Hiking, mountain biking, backpacking, on the lake, in-line skating, on snow (he was a pretty good skier!) or on the rocks. He made major contributions to the trail work at Rattlesnake and some great routes as well, both there and at other local crags, particularly at Emigrant. He was a great belay slave as well; it was like he always knew my moves—when I was sketchin' and when I could do it even if I didn't think I could. More than one hard route I have done was only because he "could tell I was on" and forced me to do it. He was always right.

His goofy penchant for mix-ups as well as his enthusiasm and enjoyment of even the most miserable bivvy forever flows through the chalk bags of all of us who knew and climbed with Jim Davis.

— Jerry Messinger, April 26, 2005

Pete Maniaci working a little left of the crux move to *Other Kids* (5.10d).
Photo: Greg Orton

Acknowledgments

Any climbing team who has faced an unclimbed wall for the first time knows the fear experienced by the author who faces the blank pages of unwritten text. I would like to extend a special thank you to the following people without whom, this guide would not have been possible.

Jerry Messinger, for the Rogue climbing history. Most of the original route descriptions for Rattlesnake, Emigrant, and Mount Ashland was drafted by and edited in collaboration with Jerry Messinger and Jim Davis.

Jim Davis (1965-2002), much of Jim's energy, words, and hopefully vision are reflected in the descriptions of this guide.

Don and Dylan Ransom, for updates and history of Rabbit Ears, the Ashland Boulders, and Greensprings.

Darryl Kasmussen for helping with the Rabbit Ears updates.

Bill NewComb for first ascent edits to Rattlesnake.

Joe Chaves, for providing a history and updates of Greensprings, Rabbit Ears, and Pilot Rock.

Shawn Tierny and Kelly Rice of the Access Fund. Each year the access fund and its sponsors (http://accessfund.org) help to support Adopt-A-Crag Day events on the Rogue to help show climber involvement with resource issues.

Mica Cardillo, Jim Hammerle, and Darryl Kasmussen for organizing local Adopt-A-Crag events. Special thanks to the Ashland Outdoor Store, McKenzie Outfitters (Medford), Metolius, and Petzl for their support in local events as well.

Mica Cardillo, Jim Hammerle, and Bill NewComb for their involvement in monitoring Peregrine falcons.

Dave Peterson (retired U.S. Fish and Wildlife Biologist). Dave has been instrumental in helping to bridge the gap and reduce barriers between climbers and land managers in western Oregon.

Larry Broeker, U.S. Forest Service, for geologic information

Special Thanks to Gilberto d' Urso of Mountain 'N Air Books.

Preface

My interest in covering climbs in the Rogue region began while I was helicopter rappelling at the Merlin helibase. This is where I met Jerry Messinger. At that time Jerry was working out during breaks on holds anchored to the side of his van. The end of each day found him working on new lines at Rattlesnake. Jerry and I had both just put out separate small guides. I was surprised by the interest generated by those two guides. Shortly after, I worked with Jerry, Jim Davis, the Ransoms, Joe Chaves, and Chuck Porter to cover the Rogue in the 2001 Rock Climbing Southwest Oregon guide.

This version of the guide includes many topo revisions that I hope make it easier to use. I have also worked with Alfred Watson to cover some of the roped climbing occurring on the coast in the last 5 years. Interest in climbing in the Rogue region has grown since 2001. The Rattlesnake crag in particular attracts state-wide attention for having a high density of challenging routes. And some of the more remote crags such as Rabbit Ears and Pilot Rock attract climbers looking to broaden their experience. In addition, gyms have opened in both Ashland and Medford introducing new climbers into the sport at a younger age.

The Climbing Western Oregon Guide series represents a lifetime of work by many individuals over several climbing careers. Each time a climber makes a first ascent they leave a legacy that others will later attempt to follow. It is important that this legacy is not lost. It is also important that those who follow recognize that the climbing legacy involves more than "just making the moves."

Beyond the moves, is a balance and rhythm of body, mind, and spirit. The further a climber moves from the known into the unknown, as he does when he moves between anchors or climbs a new route, the stronger this balance brcomes. Moving through the unknown becomes the essence of climbing "beyond the moves". Climbing's future will always be lead by those exploring the unknown.

Finally, the future of climbing on the Rogue will be influenced by how each climber, regardless of experience, takes ownership in self-managing our sport. Historically climbers have been responsible for themselves. As our interests in an area grows so does the potential for impacts to our climbing environment. Taking steps that protect the climbing environment should be as much a part of climbing as tying into your rope.

— *Greg Orton, 2005*

The Rogue River Valley

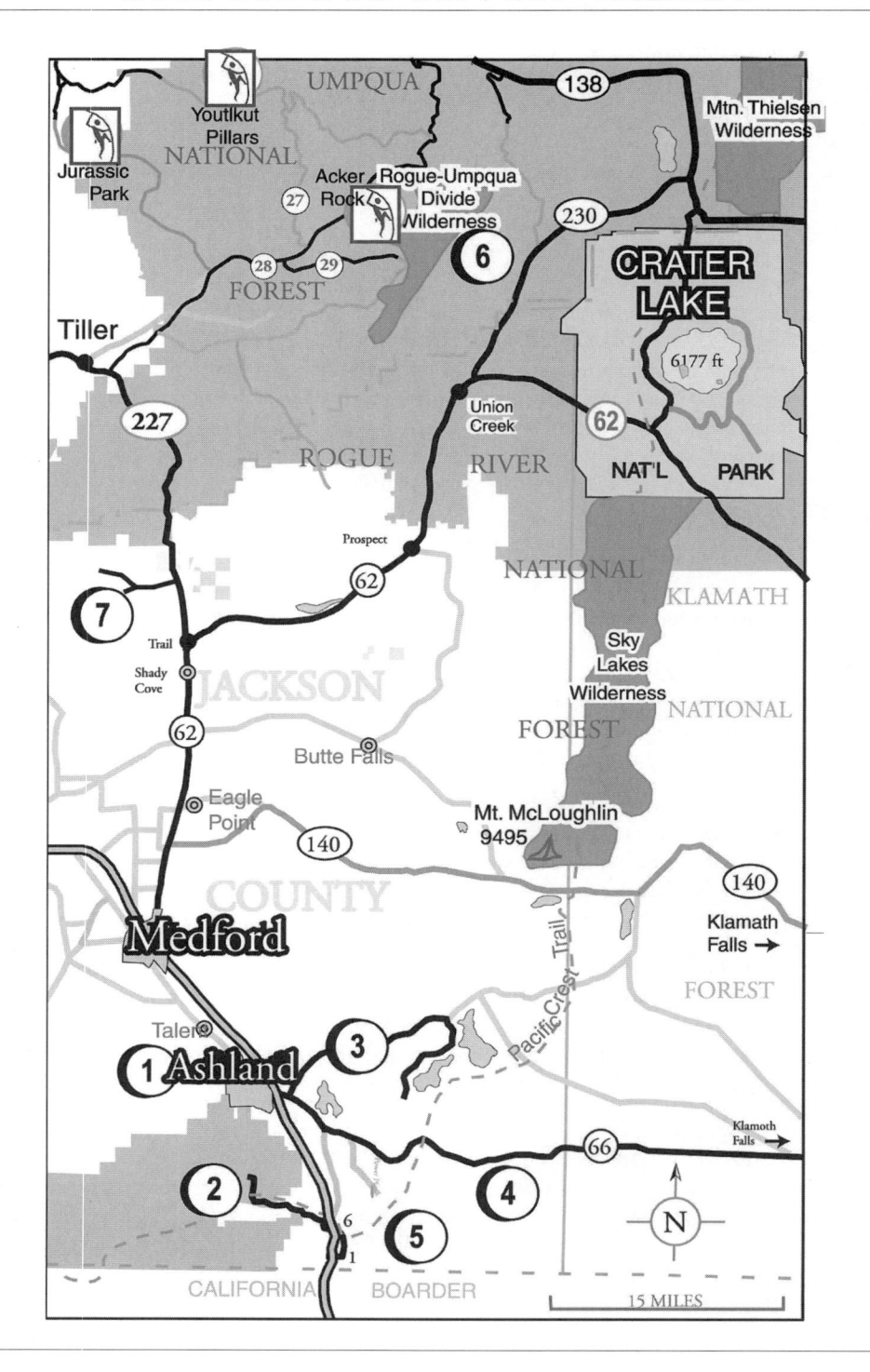

CONTENTS:

ROGUE

History	*xvi*
Geology	*xxvi*
Environmental Issues	*xxxvi*
Safety	*xi*
Climbing Ethics	*xliv*
Route Descriptions	*xlvi*

1 Ashland Boulders ... 49
Dilan Ranson

2 Mount Ashland ... 65
Jerry Messinger and Jim Davis

3 Emigrant Lake ... 69
Jerry Messinger and Jim Davis
- Poison Oak Wall ... 73
- Aqua Walland Aqua Cave ... 80

4 Greensprings ... 85
Jerry Messinger and J. Davis, J. Chaves, M. Kerr-Valentic
- Left Section ... 87
- Middle Section ... 92
- Right Section ... 93

5 Pilot Rock ... 97
Joe Chaves, Chuck Potter and Jim Davis

6 Rabbit Ears ... 105
Don Ranson, J. Messinger, J. Davis, Joe Chaves, Darryl Rasmussen

7 Rattlesnake ... 121
Jerry Messinger and Jim Davis
- Aurora Butress ... 126
- Orange Wall ... 130
- The Cathedral ... 134

8. South Coast ... 163
Alfred Watson

Seasonal Closures for Raptors
(January 1st—until fledged)
Mushroom Towers/Rattlesnake
Boise Cascade (541) 776-6684
Medford BLM(541) 440-4930
Rabbit Ears
Rogue River NF (541) 560-3400
Pilot Rock
Ashland BLM(541) 618-2499

On the left upper corner: John Rodriguez leading Start of *Hairway to Stevan* (5.10c). Don Asay

Southern Oregon Coast

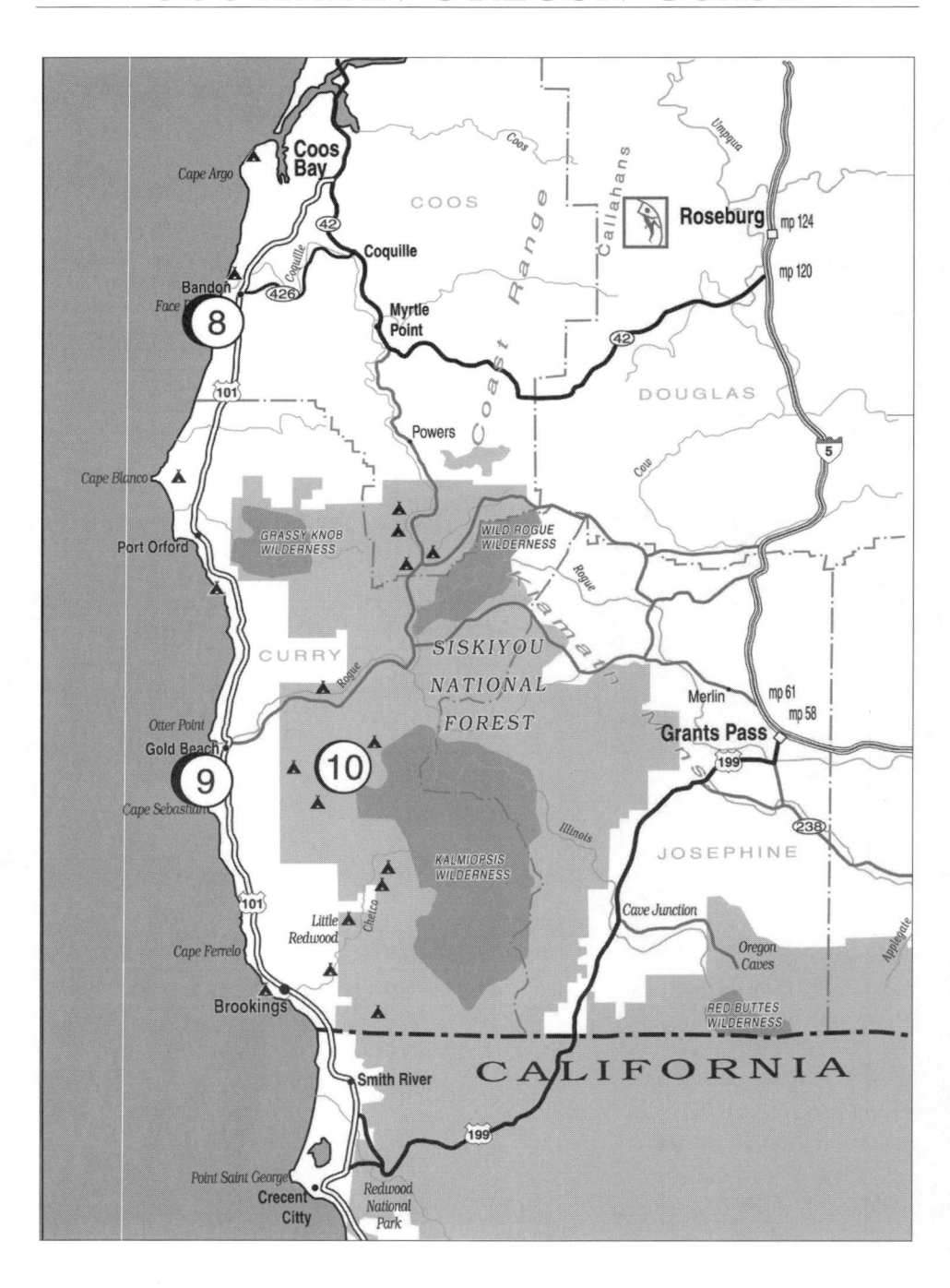

CONTENTS

OREGON COAST

8 Bandon Needles   164
Greg Orton
    Sunset Boulder   165
    Face Rock Boulder   166
    Haystack Boulder   168

9 Gold Beach Area   170
Alfred Watson
    Kissing Rock   172
    Myers Beach   174

10 Pyramid Peak   178
Alfred Watson

Mandy Bucey (at age 10) climbing to the left of *Bugoff* (5.6). Greg Orton

The Rogue River Valley

Other Attractions   The primary source of income to the Rogue Valley is Tourism, Agriculture, and Forestry. Some of the attractions to the Rogue Valley include Ashland's three Shakespearean theaters (February - October), Eagle Point's only operating water-powered grist mill east of the Mississippi River, Crater Lake National Park, and Oregon Caves to the west. There are also several excellent wineries located in the Rouge Valley.

Medford is located 4.5 hours south of Portland, 2 hours from Crater Lake National Park, 2.5 hours south of Eugene, 1.5 hours south of Roseburg. Medford is the hub for air travel into Oregon south of Eugene.

Travel Distances   Travel times to other select areas:

Castle Crags*	1.5 hours
Callahans*	2.0 hours
Acker Rock*	2.0 hours
Williamson	2.5 hours
Gold Beach	3.0 hours
Smith Rock	4.0 hours

* may require a 3/4 mile hike or greater.

Equipment Retailers   Suppliers of climbing gear in the Ashland/Medford area are McKenzie Outfitters in Medford, Ashland Outdoor Sports, and Ashland Mountain Supplies.

Climbing Clubs   Southern Oregon University Outdoor Program
Ashland Youth Climbing Program
Asland High School Climbing Club

Climbing Gyms   Southern Oregon University Rock Gym (Ashland)
Rogue Rock Gym (Medford)

Web Links   AccessFund.org
Aycp.org
Cascadiaclimbers.com
ClimbSWoregon.com
RockClimbing.com
RogueRock.com
http://ors.alpineclub.org

> "Life is not a problem to be solved but a reality to be experienced."
> —*Kierkgaard*

Rogue

Introduction

Rock climbing continues to be a popular outdoor sport that requires agility, strength, balance, and concentration. On the technical side, it requires an understanding of route finding, ropes, and protective hardware necessary to manage the risks. On a personal level, it requires balance of mind, spirit, and trust to accept the risks. Most importantly, it requires a willingness of experienced climbers to mentor those who would like to climb.

This guide is the third of a three-part series covering rock climbing in Western Oregon. Its purpose is to provide a record of established routes in the Rogue Valley and South Coast. It is intended for experienced climbers.

This series is the combined effort of many climbers. The editor has not climbed every route in this guide. Therefore, there is no guarantee to its accuracy.

HISTORY

A Climber's Guide to Oregon, written in 1968 by Nicholas A. Dodge, provided the first recorded history of rock climbing in Oregon. Prior to 1968, and through the 1970s, rock-climbing skills were being developed through mountaineering. Equipment was less developed for rock than it is today. The goal was to reach the summit climbing from the ground up. Climbing often involved aid, long leads, on routes that were extremely run-out by today's standards and more complex. Today, mountaineering and rock climbing often have little in common with one another. Risks that were at one time perceived as acceptable are now viewed by many as unsafe. A technical evolution in climbing shoes, specialized workouts, and the top-down style of climbing has pushed rock climbing beyond what was once considered possible. As with any sport, change, no matter how minor, can result in significant losses and gains. Today it is common for a new climber to learn the skills to climb beyond 5.10 while toproping in a gym, before moving onto rock with minimal experience in mountaineering, rope handling, lead climbing, or route-finding.

> "Do not follow the footsteps of the men of old; Seek what they sought."
> — *Basho*

Jerry Messinger inside Rainy Day Cave, Rattlesnake. Greg Orton

The Early Years

The 1921 ascent of Rabbit Ears on the Rogue by White and Layton is the first recorded rock climb in western Oregon. During this period and into the 1970s routes were established on-site and completely on lead. Fixed anchors were placed while on lead using a star bit drill. They climbed in stiff mountaineering boots that provided little, if any, support for edging. While climbing technique was important, it was probably less important than the climber's ability to read the rock.

> **Wearing mountaineering boots, routes were established on-site and completely on lead.**

Climbing gear had evolved little during this period. Mountaineering boots and Converse tennis shoes were common footwear. 5.8 was pushing the envelope and a leader's ability to read the rock for acceptable routes remained paramount.

Climbing activity in the 1960s was focused on pushing class-4 climbing at Pilot Rock. The obvious west gully route was most likely climbed by early Siskiyou inhabitants. The first recorded technical ascent in the Pilot Rock area was Jim Scott and Bob Ekstrand's first ascent of The Pinnacle chimney crack just 200 yards to the southeast of Pilot Rock (Dodge 1968). Three years later Pilot Rock became Scott Schmidt's obsession when he explored every potential class-4 face, ridge, and chute.

The 1960-'70s

During the 1970s, all of Oregon's attention was focused on Smith Rock, EBs revolutionized climbing footwear, and climbers began pushing the 5.10 ceiling. There was little if any route development on the Rogue during this period. Nicholas A. Dodge republished an updated version of his 1968 *A Climber's Guide to Oregon* covering both mountaineering and rock climbing in Oregon. This guide was a was a monumental achievement by anyone's standards.

The 1980s

In the early 1980s, Fire (pronounced "fee ray") climbing shoes replaced the EBs of the 1970s. By the traditional standards of the time, only the impossible faces remained to challenge climbers at Smith Rocks. Smith Rock climbers began challenging traditional ground-up ethics to establish a top-down style which allowed climbers to practice their routes before leading them. While controversial at the time, acceptance of establishing routes top-down help push climbers beyond the limits of the traditional standards and had a profound affect on climbing nationwide.

Introduction   xix

John Asay, moving left over the roof onto Ren (5.10b). Greg Orton

Rogue

The 1980s saw Rouge climbers exploring new routes closer to home. The cracks at Greensprings were starting to be explored with an eye for maintaining a ground-up, protect-on-lead ethic as was the ice polished Lower Apron of Rabbit Ears where Randy Benham, Don Ransom, and Michael Lee were focussing their efforts. In the latter half of the 1980s Dan Higgins was exploring new routes at Mount Ashland, Greenspings, and Emigrant Lake.

At Smith Rock climbers began challenging the ethic of pioneering routes on lead.

The 1990s

As we entered into the 1990s, rock climbing has continued to evolve from its origins of mountaineering and "traditional" climbing. Shoes continued to improve and climbing gyms were established. Not only did gyms and homemade climbing walls help with specialized workouts, they also allowed climbers to workout during the winter months to increase peak performance during the climbing months.

With the exception of a few diehard traditionalists, climbing had taken on entirely new dimensions. The decade saw an explosion in new routes in western Oregon. We also saw a continued challenge to traditional ethics as some climbers contrived to blur the line between free and aid climbing by modifying the rock to create holds needed to make their climbs.

In the Rogue Valley, the first half of the 1990s saw an increased interest in establishing new lines at Greensprings and Emigrant Lake. The efforts of Dan Higgins and Don Ransom were later complemented by up and coming new faces to the Rogue climbing scene. The incredible efforts of Gavin Ferguson, Jim Smallwood, Cory Jones, Randy Benham, Bill Newcomb, Jim Davis, Jerry Messinger, Joe Chaves, and Chuck Porter defined Rogue climbing in the '90s. By the time 2000 came around the intensity of which Jerry Messinger and Joe Chaves were climbing was perhaps unmatched by any other effort at anytime in western Oregon. Jerry Messinger who was pioneering new sport routes at every location on the Rogue later teamed up with Bill Newcomb, Jim Davis, and others at Rattlesnake. By the end of the decade there were over 100 new sport routes at Rattlesnake. Over a quarter of these are rated in the 5.12 and 5.13 range and more than half are 5.11 or greater making Rattlesnake second only to Smith Rock for having the largest concentration of technical sport routes in Oregon.

Joelle Watson, leads *Never Been Kissed* (5.6), Kissing Rock, Gold Beach. Greg Orton

At about the same time Rattlesnake was being developed, Joe Chaves and Chuck Porter pioneered several ambitious, multi-pitch routes on the south face columns of Pilot Rock. These included *Crash Landing* (5.8), *RoundAbout* (5.10d), *StepUp* (5.10b), and the classic *Magic Blocks* (5.11a). *Magic Blocks*, remains a test piece for local climbers.

Rabbit Ears was receiving renewed attention in the latter half of the '90s as Don Randsom returned to Rabbit Ears with son Dylan. Together they establish several new lines on the Lower Apron, in 'traditional' ground-up style while setting anchors on lead. Chaves and Porter pioneered several additional multi-pitch routes on the East Ear.

Several climbing guides for the Rogue were produced in the '90s. These guides in order of distribution were *Rock Climbing in Southern Oregon*, 1991 by Jerry Messinger; *A Climber's Guide to Emigrant Lake and The Greensprings*, by Chris Elder; *A Climber's Guide to the Greensprings Climbing Area*, 1995 by Mahlon Kerr-Velentic; and *Rattlesnake*, 1998 by Jerry Messinger and Jim Davis. With the fast-pace of route setting during this period guides were going out-of-date as quickly as they were coming out.

2000 and Toward the Future

Unfortunately the Rogue lost Jim Davis to a mountaineering accident in 2002. Jerry Messinger, Joe Chaves, and Bill Newcomb continue to pioneer new lines on the Rogue. Recently Joe completed perhaps his most ambitious route, *The Prize* (5.11b) on the Umpqua's Old Man Rock, and has several new ascents at both Greensprings and the Lower Apron of Rabbit Ears.

A new climbing gym has opened in Ashland at the Southern Oregon University Outdoor Center. The *Ashland Youth Climbing Club* is active at the Outdoor Center, a High School climbing club was recently started in Ashland, and a new gym is scheduled to open in Medford in the spring of 2005. As climbers continue to become involved at a younger age benchmarks that where realized in the '90s will be overcome by a new generation of climbers.

Introduction xxiii

Bill Newcomb assisting the Forest Service with Peregrine monitoring and banding in Trail Creek. Greg Orton

Rogue

CLIMBING SEASON

Average annual rainfall varies from north to south with the climate becoming dryer as you travel south. Medford, which is centrally located in the Rogue Valley, averages 19 inches of rainfall each year. This is thirty percent less rainfall than Eugene just 160 miles to the north. Winter average temperatures range from 38 to 46 degrees and average summer temperatures are in the 70s. Eighty percent of the precipitation delivered to the Rogue Valley occurs between October and April with the three wettest months occurring in November, December and January.

Typically, the climbing season in the lower elevations of the Rogue can extend from the early April into the middle of October. However, in the winter, with a couple days of dry weather it is not uncommon to find someone out climbing on warmer south facing routes and overhangs around Rattlesnake, Emigrant Lake, and the Ashland Boulders. On the coast, climbing is actually preferable during winter months when there is less wind and fog. A foggy winter day in the Rogue Valley can be an indicator of clear warm weather on both the coast and nearby foothills.

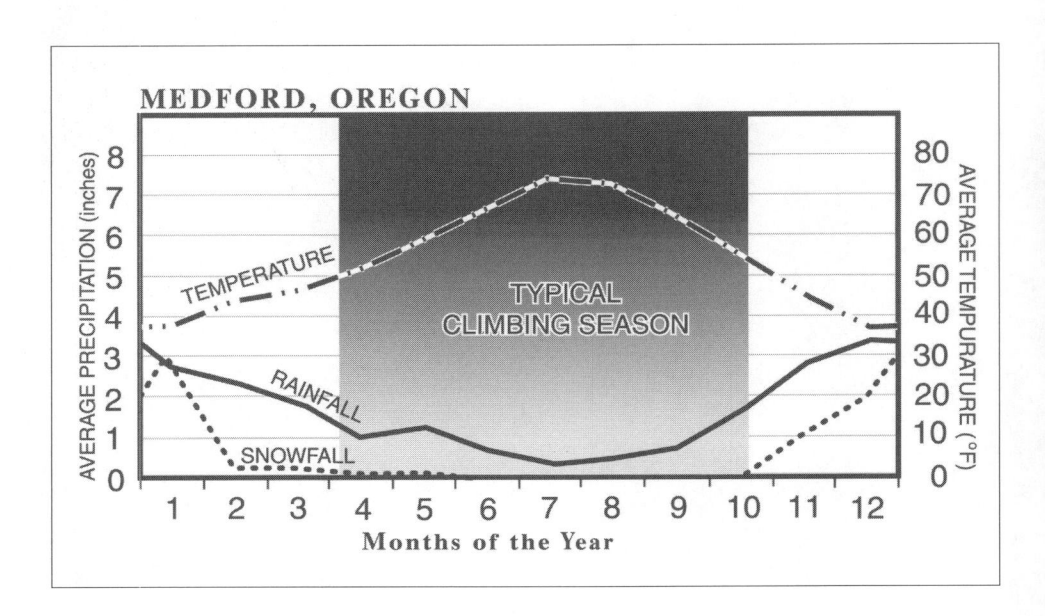

"The moment of terror marks the beginning of conscious life, Mike, so take the *"No Fear"* sticker off your truck."
— Mark Twight

Early spring day. Brandon Knapp in the Cathedral, Rattlesnake. Greg Orton

"Faint to my ears cam the gathering rumor of all lands: the springing and the dying, the song and the weeping, and the slow everlasting groan of overburdened stone."

- J. R. R. Tolkien

GEOLOGY

A climbing guide to western Oregon would not be complete without a discussion of the nature of the rocks themselves. The geology of western Oregon is diverse, complex, and as interesting to study as it is to climb. Several excellent publications on the subject are *Geology of Oregon* by Elizabeth and William Orr, and Ewart M. Baldwin, and *Roadside Geology of Oregon* by David D. Alt and Donald W. Hyndman.

Oregon's coastal and Cascade mountains formed under techtonic forces. A rift zone in the Pacific Ocean causes spreading of the Oceanic Plates. As these dense basaltic plates are pushed eastward they collide with the lighter continental plate. The force of this collision pushes the Pacific Oceanic plates under the North American continent until it becomes molten and rises towards the surface.

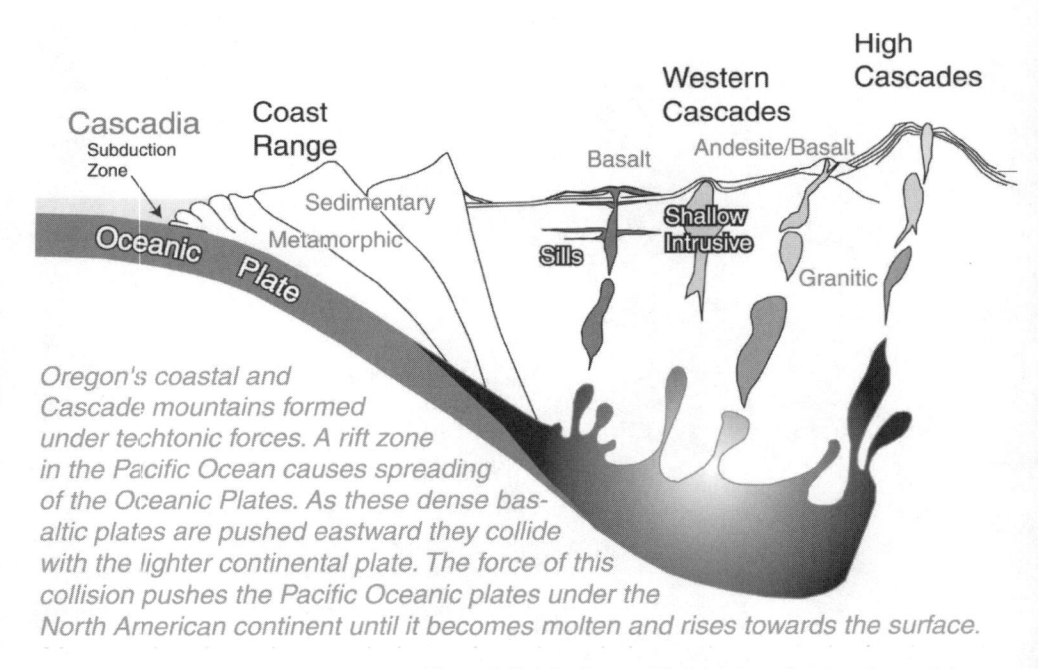

Figure 1: Subduction and the creation of rock and mountains.

Coast Range Province — In the Pacific, a huge rift zone splits the ocean bottom into tectonic plates that drift in a easterly direction. When these plates collide with the lighter continental crust of Oregon they are forced downward while sediment and rocks riding ontop the ocean floor are scraped off and accreted to Oregon's coast (figure 1). This collision between the oceanic and continental plates occurs at a rate of 1 inch per year. The force of impact buckles the coast range into north-south trending ridges, and dramatic sea cliffs, particularly towards the south where the subduction zone is closest to Oregon's shore.

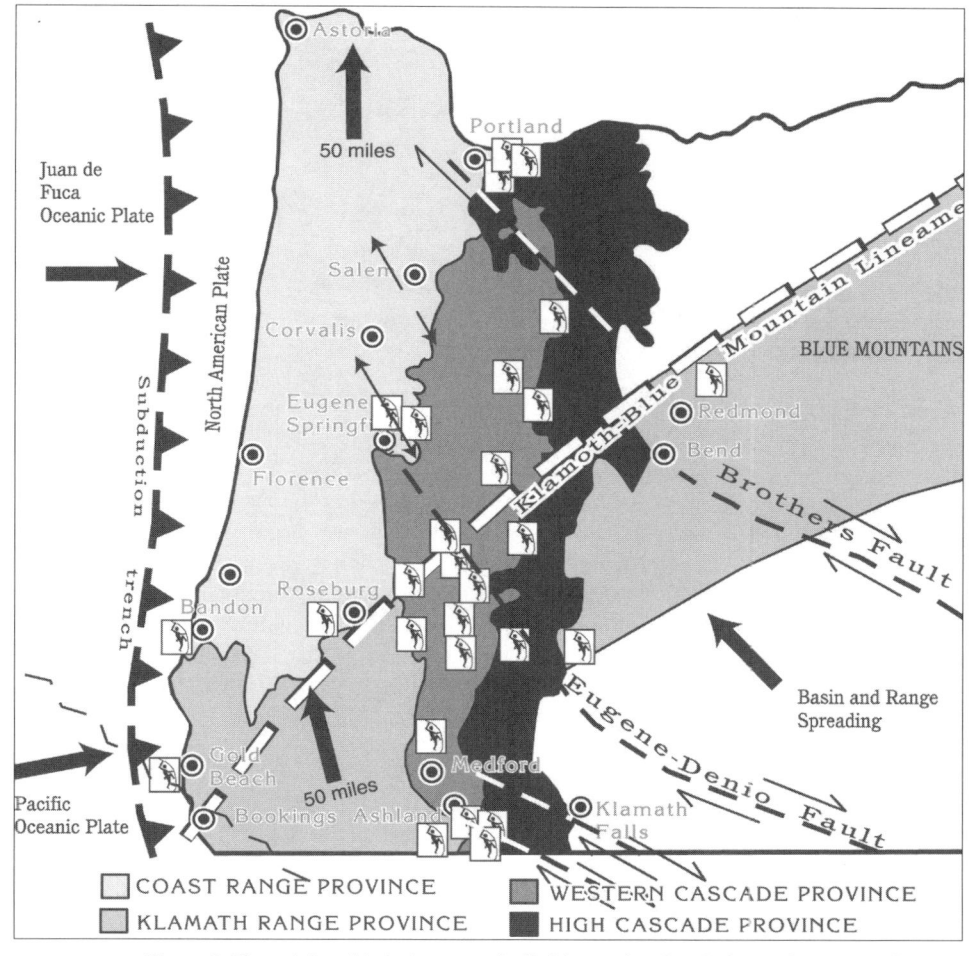

Figure 2: The relationship between rock climbing and techtonic forces in western Oregon.

Sea Stacks Only 35 miles from the subduction zone, Cape Blanca rises at a rate of 1 inch every 3 years. This accelerated force has lifted ancient marine terraces of sand and gravel, from 20 to over 50 feet in thickness, to an elevation as high as 1,600 feet between Coos Bay and Port Orford. The constant action of waves during high tide cuts the lower terrace into 80 foot cliffs and exposed rocks and small islands that ride as residuum on top the ocean floor as it collides with the Oregon coast. These rocks and islands are further sculpted into the enchanting sea stack formations, of which the Bandon needles are perhaps most memorable.

Metavolcanics - Metavolcanic sea stacks form from volcanic rocks that have been placed under tremendous pressure and temperatures.

Kissing Rock located just south of Gold Beach is a sea stack of metavolcanic tuff and breccia.

These forces reformed and recrystalize the rock giving it a harder and more weather resistant nature than the original rock. Blueschist for example, prized for its weather resistance, has been quarried and used as riprapping in constructing breakwaters. Bandon's Sunset Boulder is a blueschist and provides some of the better climbing opportunity the coast. Just south of Gold Beach, Kissing Rock and Meyers Rock provide additional opportunity for serious climbing. On Kissing Rock large jugs of volcanic breccia have been welded together providing excellent overhung climbing.

Caution should be taken when climbing sea stacks, where rock quality can deteriorate quickly towards the top of rocks. Although one can find several weathered bolt lines up several of these sea stacks, handholds can be marginal. Most sea stack formations are better suited for bouldering around the base than technical climbing.

Introduction   xxix

Klamath Mountain Province
The Klamath and Blue Mountains are the oldest formation in Oregon. They once formed the western shore along the Idaho-Nevada border. The rest of Oregon did not appear until about 40 million years ago, long after the dinosaurs. Prior to this, a rift valley formed in today's Basin and Range. One theory is that this rift has pushed the Klamath-Blue Mountain Range from its original north-south position into their present position, forming the Klamath-Blue Mountain Lineament (figure 2). This lineament of thicker crust most likely extends south as far as the South Umpqua Block faulting beginning about 13 million years ago and a northward push of the Pacific Plate in the south has since pulled the western part of Oregon to the north. This northward movement is evident today by a 50-mile northward deflection in the Columbia River and Olympic Peninsula west of the Cascades.

Granitic Intrusions
Granitic rocks are formed from magma that has mixed with the crust and cooled before reaching the surface. The oldest granitic exposures in Oregon are the quartz monzonite and granodiorite of Mount Ashland and the Ashland Boulders. Large square pink feldspar crystals and coarse texture help identify this type of granitic rock. They are very resistant to weathering.

The quartz monzonite and granodiorite of Mount Ashland and the Ashland Boulders are expamples of granitic rocks found in the Klamoth Mountain Province.

Rogue

| Western Cascade Province | About 35 million years ago, subduction of the ocean floor shifted west from the Idaho-Nevada boarder to where it is today just 50 miles off Oregon's coast. Five million years later, the subducting ocean floor melted and rose through weaknesses in the overlying crust to form the Western Cascade. Magma that reaches the surface without much mixing will form lava of basalt low in silica and high in iron. Volcanoes that expel basalt lava are low in profile and have a low resiliency to weathering. Today, little remains of the Western volcanoes, which have since become uplifted and eroded forming the west-facing ramp where the Rogue River Basins has formed. The Western Cascade, most recognized as a basaltic formation, provides little opportunity for rock climbing. |

| High Cascade Province | As the oceanic plates subduct under Oregon it travels downward at an angle to a depth of some six miles and 100 miles eastward. At these depths the heat and pressure remelts the plate into molten magma. Magma, when molten, becomes lighter than the material above and begins rising up through weakness in the overlying continent. As the magma rises it can remelt and mix with other rocks and material in the earths crust.

The High Cascades are primarily characterized by the formation of andesite. Magma passing through the Klamath-Blue Mountain Lineament became even more siliceous, providing the Trail Creek area with the Rhyodacitic tuffaceaous (compact volcanic ash high in pinkish feldspar minerals and quartz) cliffs of Rattlesnake and the dacite of Rabbit Ears in the upper Rogue. When more mixing occurs as the rising magma passes through the thicker crustal rock of the Klamath-Blue Mountain Lineament, silica and acidic rich minerals (rhyolitic minerals) become incorporated into the molten mix. Magmas high in silica will become less viscous, and more explosive than those with less silica. Lava flows from magma can range from basalt (basic) to rhyolites (acidic) depending on the types of feldspar and amount of silica they contain. Basalt flows easily and spreads out into thin, flat flows. Rhyolite has the highest amount of silica and flows more like toothpaste resulting in thick often dome like flow deposits. Smith Rock is an example of rock that was deposited by a rhyolitic volcano. Rhyolitic rocks can be very resilient to weathering. |

ROCK TYPES

| Sandstone | Sandstone is developed when weathered sands or ash are deposited in a body of water. The rock surrounding Emigrant Lake is a coarse grained to pebbly volcanic sandstone ranging from 40 to 90 feet in |

height. This sandstone is derived from volcanic sands with coloring from iron oxidation. The formation has weathered into rounded bouldery formations.

Emigrant Lake sandstone

Columnar Structures

Greensprings and Pilot Rock provide exceptional crack and face climbing on columnar structures. Climbs at these formations are approximately 100 feet in height at Greensprings to 300 feet at Pilot Rock. The rock at Greensprings is a fine-grained hornblende granodiorite that most likely formed as a shallow intrusive. Pilot Rock is a volcanic plug where columnar structures can be weakly situated in places. The stability of columns can change from one year to the next. Prismatic structures form when magma cools and contracts under ideally uniform conditions to allow a regular jointing pattern. These four to six-sided prisms form perpendicular to their cooling surfaces. Therefore, columns such as Greensprings that cooled slowly below the surface in sills or lacoliths (magma that was injected and cooled between two sedimentary layers) have vertical columns. Columns that form in thin dikes or at the outer edge of volcanic vents, such as Pilot Rock, can range from vertical to horizontal.

On top the Pilot Rock columns.

Volcanic Tuff and Sedimentary Volcanics

Rattlesnake was formed from glowing tuff and volcanic avalanches. The hardness of these deposits is the result of the degree of heating and alteration that took place after they were deposited. The quality of this rock can vary within the same unit. Climbs at Rattlesnake range from 80 to 150 feet in height.

Weathered volcanic tuff at Rattlesnake.

Volcanic Plugs	Rabbit Ears and Pilot Rock formed from magma that cooled in place before being exhumed from the ground. Magma that formed in the necks of volcanoes, vents, and dikes, cooled slowly forming dense weather resistant rock. This harder core rock has been exposed through erosional processes.

The rock in the upper portion of Rabbit Ears is a massive, sparsely jointed, partially welded volcanic tuff-breccia of andesitic or dacitic composition. Rock quality increases at the lower apron where it has become polished by snow and ice movement.

Pilot Rock was formed as a shallow-intrusive volcanic plug that formed huge prismatic columns. The rock is a columnar dacite containing hornblende and calcite crystals.

Erosion has exposed the volcanic core that formed Pilot Rock.

Rogue

ROCK QUALITY

How rocks formed can have an effect their resiliency to weathering. Cracks and layers provide pathways to moisture which helps to break down rock. The hardness of the rock can also vary. Volcanic tuffs (uniform grains), volcanic breccias (conglomerates) are deposited as glowing avalanches or air fall which can result in interbedding of softer rock and layered weaknesses in the rock structure. Massive rocks that form as a consolidated unit can have cracks as their zone of weakness or can also have large pockets of weaker material with in the same unit.

The mineral make-up of the rock can also affect the rock's resiliency to weathering. Silica is much more weather resistant than other minerals. Rhyolites, rhyodacites, and granodiorite, dacites contain quartz and feldspars associated with the more weather resistant rhyolite. Andesites and basalt will be low in quartz and contain feldspars that are less resistant to weathering. Andesite and basalt rarely provides quality rock for climbing in western Oregon.

Heat and pressure can increase or decrease the rock's resiliency to weathering. This can occur when successive deposits, faulting, and subduction bury a rock, or when mineral rich steam is injected into the rock. A beneficial effect of the weathering process is the formation of a hard surface layer called a varnish or patina. This is caused by minerals in the formation being wicked or carried to the surface by moisture. These minerals of iron, magnesium, manganese oxides and hydroxides form a very hard, dark plating in the surface inch or so of the rock. Drying and oxidation at the surface hardens these minerals into a shallow crust. A patina can take tens of thousands of years to form. The color and thickness of the patina can indicate how long the surface has been exposed and be an indicator of the rock's stability.

In volcanic rocks texture is influenced by how long it took the magma to cool. The longer the cooling time the larger the crystals will be that form. Magmas that cool slowly below the surface will have coarser textures than those that form as lava flows and cool quickly.

Climbers on the first pitch (5.10b) of *Magic Blocks*, Pilot Rock. Greg Orton

> "The goal of life is
> living in agreement with Nature"
> — *Zeno of Elea*

ENVIRONMENTAL ISSUES

Climbs in western Oregon are remote and for the most part in an unimproved natural state. For over five decades climbers before us made it their responsibility to limit their impacts and protect their climbing environment. It is our turn.

Wildlife, regardless of how common or rare, or their political and social status needs to be understood and respected. Eagles, redtail hawks, and falcons should all be treated with respect. It is common to see these magnificent birds while out climbing.

Peregrine Falcon

After several decades of declining population, Peregrine falcons are again becoming common on southwest Oregon rocks. In 1999, the Federal Government down listed Peregrine from "Threatened and Endangered" to "Threatened." The State of Oregon has chosen to keep Peregrine listed as "Threatened and Endangered."

Between 1995 and 2000 the number of known pairs in Oregon doubled from 41 to 83. By 2003, eyries (nest sites) in Oregon had increased to 112. Over 85% of these occur on the side west of the Cascade and coast range. There was a 71% increase in occupied nesting sites during this period. Of these 51% to 90% successfully fledged depending on the year surveyed.

Recreational Climbing Affect on Raptors

Rock climbing in southwest Oregon greatly increased during the years when falcons were relatively scarce or absent. As Peregrine numbers increase, falcons are re-inhabiting cliffs that have become favorite climbing routes. Climbers are also continuing to explore new rock faces with existing nesting sites. Climbers have the potential to directly impact falcons and other raptors during nesting. Unlike disturbances caused by recreationalists such as hikers and picnickers, a climbing party may be on a rock face for long periods and can cause nest failure if the nesting pair become disturbed for long periods.

Peregrines do not construct nest and will hatch their eggs in the fine gravels on ledges, referred to as an eyrie.

Chicks can be sensitive to climber disturbances until they have left the nesting ledge.
Photo: Greg Orton

Falcons and other raptors display varying degrees of sensitivity to disturbance. Raptors nesting in remote areas tend to be relatively intolerant of humans in their territories, while others that choose to nest where they are exposed to regular disturbances, are usually more tolerant of humans. In general raptors are much more sensitive to people above their nest sites than to people below or across. Climbers should avoid entering these areas from February until two weeks after the young have fledged (left the nest). The courtship and incubation period is the most critical time for birds of prey, and disturbance by humans can cause nest abandonment. This period can extend from March into June depending on the season. The time of fledging can vary from year to year. In most cases the young can be expected to fledge sometime in June.

Peregrine in flight.
Greg Orton

Raptors screaming at climbers, taking avoidance flights, and/or dive-bombing climbers who have come too close to the nesting site are typical responses caused by climbers. Peregrine, sounding a territorial alarm, create a loud "CACK, CACK, CACK," that some compare to the sound of a cackling seagull. When the chicks are old enough to leave the nest, (referred to as having "fledged"), they are still dependent on the adults for their food but less susceptible to disturbance. Prior to the young fledging, climbers may assume cackling birds a sign to leave.

Become Aware

Seasonal wildlife closures affect access into Rabbit Ears, the Mushroom Towers at Rattlesnake, and to the east and south face of Pilot Rock. Closures are in effect vary from January up until two weeks after the young have fledged from the nest, or monitoring determines the site to be inactive. Closures can be extended to July 31 when there is a lack of monitoring information to make a determination or a lack of public interest.

Seasonal wildlife closures affect access at Rabbit Ears, Rattlesnakes Mushroom Towers, and the south face of Pilot Rock.

Both the climbing population and the mobility of climbers are increasing. There exists a need to provide current site-specific information to increasing numbers of climbers from outside the local area. Climbers need to be apprized of pertinent restrictions before they visit raptor-sensitive areas. The ever-increasing complexity of issues, legal mandates, and resource limitations faced by managers, have made it difficult for climbers to stay current on issues.

A Need For Better Information

The Access Fund maintains a list of seasonal closures to climbing areas throughout the country at AccessFund.org. ClimbSWoregon.com tracks local climbing closures, access issues, and volunteer monitoring projects

Personal Responsibility

Historically, climbers in remote areas have climbed under an ethic of low impact and low visibility. Ethics are as much a part of climbing as the climb itself. They evolved to preserve the essential elements of the climbing experience. These elements include climbing a rock on its own terms while not adversely affecting the rock or rock ecology. However, information on sensitive sites was often unavailable. In recent years, better communications between the Willamette National Forest, the City of Eugene, and climbers has increased our ability to continue to self-manage and take ownership in resource protection.

Future actions that land managers can take to improve our ability to self-regulate and continue to protect the rock ecology are:

1) Continue to recognize climbing as a recreational opportunity that has a history in western Oregon.
2) Work to form partnerships with local climbers and national climbing resource groups such as the Access Fund and The Mountaineers.
3) Be open to providing climbers with specific information on areas that are sensitive to climbing.
4) Continue to allow climbers with the latitude to participate in conflict resolution and route management.

Climbers have a personal responsibility for accepting ownership and building partnerships that will continue to maintain and improve our climbing environment. Each year there are clean-up events, trail days, Adopt-A-Crag events, and organized monitoring efforts being conducted at climbing areas throughout Oregon. These efforts play a significant role towards helping reduce our cumulative impacts. The possibilities for future events are only limited by our imaginations. Climbers and land managers interested becoming a local contact can contact the Access Fund at http://www.accessfund.com.

Photo: Adopt-A-Crag cleanups sponsored by local interest and the Access Fund have helped climbers build working partnerships with private land managers. From left to right: Allan Kelley, David and Dee Tvedt, Chandler Orton, Harold Hall, Greg Orton. Tim Kosderka

SAFETY

> "A climber's safety begins and ends with his efforts to avoid, control, and cope with climbing hazards. His safety being a personal matter, he must accept responsibility for himself [and his partners] when he climbs. He must know his limits and climb within them or accept the results when he goes beyond them."
> - Mountaineering: Freedom of the Hills, 1979.

Climbing has inherent risks. The risk of falling is never completely eliminated, as is the risk of having an accident while driving a car can never be completely eliminated. The art of rock climbing is learning how to manage these risks. Beginning climbers most often start out toproping climbs. In this way, the risks are reduced to the stretch of a rope, the integrity of the anchoring system, the skill of the belayer, and the ability of the climber to make the moves.

Routes in this guide are rated using the standard decimal system (refer to Route Classification). These ratings are provided to give climbers a "relative" idea of the route's difficulty. Individual safety may hinge on an understanding of the decimal system. Be aware that ratings are subjective and can vary between climbers, by climbing area, the season, and by how clean the route is at the time you climb it.

There are two types of hazards that lead to accidents:
1. Those that are human mistakes or predictable "Pilot Error", where an accident can be prevented by taking a mitigating action, and
2. Those that are random, unpredictable "Acts of God", where the only mitigation is to recognize the hazards and limit your exposure to them.

Inexperience often leads us to perceive a hazard as not being able to be mitigated. A beginning climber may fail to perceive and take ownership in hazards he creates such as a protection point that is inadequately evaluated and then fails. As one gains experience the unpredictable hazards become less.

Each climber is responsible for evaluating the integrity of his protection. Fixed anchor placement, regardless of size and quality, can become questionable over time and must be reevaluated with each climb. Also, the integrity of the rock can vary from one season to the next. If your expectations are that maintaining the route you are about to climb is someone else's responsibility; you are in the wrong sport. The only ones responsible for your safety and enjoyment are you and your partners.

Errors in This Guide and Landowner Liability

Please take the time to read the warning of possible errors that may be contained in this guide and an explanation of *Oregon law (105.665)* protecting private landowners from liability. This information is presented at the bottom of the Copyright page.

Environmental Hazards

Ticks - can be a problem in grass meadows and brush along thermal belts above valleys. When in a tick area your best avoidance is to remain on trails as much as possible. Wear mosquito/tick repellent containing DEET (leave the Skin-So-Soft at home) and check yourself for ticks. As soon as you return home, wash your clothes, and take a shower.

Rattlesnakes - are present but rarely seen in rocky south slopes of much of south Oregon. I do not know of any climbers getting bit in western Oregon. If you are, do not cut and suck. Relax, keep the bite lower than your heart, and see a doctor.

Poison Oak - is common, but avoidable. There is a lot of misinformation in the climbing community related to poison oak. Many people will develop resistance with exposure, others will not, and in many people sensitivity does not increase with exposure. My personal experience with poison oak is that I can both crush a leaf into our skin with only a minor reaction while my wife can get a severe reation from just touching my clothes. Chandler has developed a similar resistance to mine. Bottom-line, everyone reacts differently. A good weblink for more information on poison oak is http://www.waynesword.palomar.edu.

Climbing with Children

Spending time with children on the rock is an incredibly rewarding experience for both child and adult. When climbing with children there are a few additional rules to follow:

1) Have enough experienced climbers that one can be assigned to each child as needed, with never less than two adults;

2) To guarantee a child's success, do not challenge them, let them challenge themselves.

I once was asked if introducing my son to such a dangerous sport ever concerned me. This is a difficult question. Chandler, now 17, appears extremely safety conscious, something he did not inherit from his father. I also see him adapting the skills he has developed as a climber to his life. My hope is he will continue to use these skills in a variety of future situations.

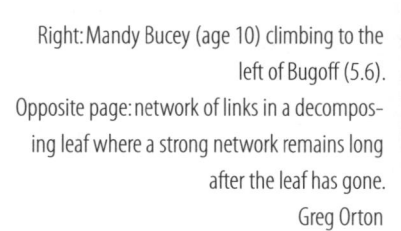

Right: Mandy Bucey (age 10) climbing to the left of Bugoff (5.6).
Opposite page: network of links in a decomposing leaf where a strong network remains long after the leaf has gone.
Greg Orton

Introduction   xliii

"An accident is a chain of events interrupted. These events are often inaccurately referred to as "near misses."

"A climber must continually evaluate the risks and hazards that determine his progress."

"...one more bolt would make it accessible to many more climbers. One more bolt would also rob it of a tremendous amount of atmosphere, excitement and challenge, of its spirit and so of its quality. It would become just another route..."

— Peter Gulyash

CLIMBING ETHICS

Climbers are known for their independence. We do not relish the idea that someone might tell us what we can climb, when we can climb, where we can climb, or how we can climb. An ethic should represent a general consensus by climbers to reduce our collective impacts and preserve the first ascent nature of an area.

It should not have to be said that it is all our responsibility to maintain the climbing areas we visit. Even if it is a first visit, we should all take responsibility to leave the approaches, belays, campsites, and parking areas in better shape than we found them. Our climbs are slowly being impacted by use. We need to remain conscious of these impacts. One cigarette butt at the base of a climb seems insignificant until they have had time to accumulate. It is very important that we pack out all our garbage, bury our toilet paper well so that animals won't dig it up, and park our cars so that they will have the least amount of impact. If we find some trash or a cigarette butt accidentally dropped by another party, it is important that we "ALL" are willing to make the extra effort and pack it out. Increased litter is particularly a problem along access roads and remote camps during hunting season.

The Climbing Area

Trails — Properly placed access trails can be essential to reducing our impacts to an area. It is important to clearly mark access routes to reduce the amount of area disturbed as climbing parties move in and out of an area. Federal law requires an Environmental Assessment of potential impacts be made before any new trail can be constructed on public lands. However, just flagging an access route from a parking area to the rock can help reduce our disturbance. The quantity and quality of trails to each area vary. The number of trails should always be kept at a minimum. The quality of existing trails should be maintained by proper use, not cutting switchbacks and by organizing or volunteering time to trail maintenance events.

Projects	It is customary for someone working out moves on a route to mark their project by hanging red flagging on the bottom anchor. A general courtesy is that other climbers allow the individual time to work out the moves and complete a first ascent on their project. This courtesy stems from the amount of work often necessary to prepare a route for a first ascent and work out the moves. A reciprocal courtesy is that a climber establishing projects will not tie up a rock face by establishing more than one project at any one time. If you burnout on one and wish to move onto another, the first route should become open for others to attempt a first ascent.
Route Chipping	Altering the rock by chipping handholds or foot placements in routes is unacceptable. The Access Fund to their credit has taken a position against chipping, classifying the practice, "irresponsible climbing." Locally routes that have been overly chipped have been subject to being chopped by other climbers. Established routes that were climbed using chipped handholds have been designated as aid routes in this guide and represent a darker side of the free-for-all attitude of climbing in the '90s.
The Use of Chalk	Chalk is used on climbs to dry oils from the hands and increase friction. When too much chalk is used, handholds become marked. Marked routes can detract from the "first climb - route-finding experience" of the next climber. The use of chalk on climbs has become more of a bad habit than a useful aid. Once the hand oils have been dried with chalk it is only periodically needed for the remainder of the climb. If you are already in the habit of reaching for the chalk each time the adrenal glands pump, try using a chalk ball to help meter the amount of chalk you use.
Fixed Anchors	Due to the nature of the rock in our local area, cracks and crags that offer the opportunity for clean climbing without the use of fixed anchors are rare. Therefore, it is important that all new routes be established as cleanly as possible and that the integrity of established routes are maintained. Observe a clean climbing ethic - use chocks, cams, and runners when possible. Place fixed anchors as a last resort when placement of a removable anchor is not possible or the quality of the rock makes placement questionable. Never alter an established route by removing or placing additional fixed anchors without first checking with the climbers who established the route. Upgrading anchors with ones that are

stronger and/or less visible is of course encouraged, but should remain as close to the original placement as possible. This includes replacing old webbing with new, removing a bolt on route and replacing it with a stronger bolt, and adding a bolt to an established belay or rappel point (unless specified in the guide as inappropriate).

Adding additional bolts to an existing route can be extremely controversial. Realize that "run-out" is often as subjective as "well-protected." Therefore, the final decision for altering rests on agreement of the first ascent party.

Loose hangers are common. Rope tension or a beginning climber stepping on a hanger can cause a hanger to spin and loosen the nut. Nuts can be "snugged," using a wrench. However, do not over-tighten nuts to the point where the bolt begins to move outward.

Power hammers are not allowed in areas that have been designated as Wilderness or in the Pilot Rock area.

ROUTE DESCRIPTIONS

Descriptions in this guide are a compilation of unverified information gathered from many different sources. There is no guarantee to the accuracy of any of the information in this book, including topo and route descriptions, difficulty ratings, and protection ratings. Bolt placements on topos are approximations, and ratings are subjective and prone to error. I have spent countless hours and edits to reproduce a record, that is as accurate as possible in presenting the information received from climbers. Sometimes this information is obscure, incomplete, or second hand.

The routes described in this guide are rated using the Yosemite Decimal System. An attempt has been made to rate climbs to reflect the technical skill level required to make the most difficult moves on a route. Routes marked with chalk or that are first climbed by toprope can reduce or totally eliminate the element of route finding on lead. This in turn can create a tendency to down-rate a climb. Routes which require placement of traditional protection will require a different skill level than routes, which are rated the same but are protected with fixed anchors. Because rating routes is somewhat subjective, communication amongst climbers is vital to maintaining consistency. The difficulty of routes given the same rating in this guide can vary between areas and between climbing parties who provide the ratings.

Run-out, Well-protected, Over-bolted are subjective terms.

GRADE RATINGS

Climbs are also rated by grades from I to VI to express a combination of factors determining the required level of general mountaineering skill and commitment. Grade should not be confused with class, which only evaluates technical climbing difficulty. Climbs in Southwest Oregon range from Grade I to III. Unless noted all climbs in this guide are Grade I and can be completed in several hours, at the most.

Grade I - Technical portions take several hours.

Grade II - Technical portions require half a day. Many of the longer routes in this guide are considered Grade II.

Grade III - Technical portions require most of a day. Wolf Rock and Acker Rock have routes that are Considered Grade III.

CLASS RATING SYSTEM

Class 3: Easy climbing, handholds and footholds are used. The exposure is such that a beginner might feel queasy without a rope. Elementary climbing techniques are helpful. Many of the routes described as walk-offs for climbs are of this class.

Class 4: A rope is necessary for belaying from an anchor point. A leader fall from a class 4 would be serious, but climbing is not considered difficult. Protection is not usually required on the route. Some of the easier routes in this guide have been assigned Class 5 ratings but could technically be considered Class 4.

Yosemite Decimal System

Class 5.0-5.13: (with Yosemite Decimal System). Roped climbing, requiring protection along the route, as well as belays. Climbs made in this class are made without the use of aid and are termed "free climbing."

Aid

Class Ac, A0-A5: Direct aid. Stepping on hangers or using the climbing rope, slings, chocks, glued or chipped holds, expansion bolts or other anchors are necessary for physical support or aid in making an ascent. Ac is used for aid routes where holds have been chipped into the rock.

YDS	5.7	5.8	5.9	10a	10b	10c	10d	11a	11b	11c	11d	12a	12b	12c	12d	13a	13b	13c	13d	14a...
V			V0-	V0	V0+		V1		V2		V3	V4		V5	V6	V7	V8	V9		V10...
French	5a	5b	5c	6a		6b		6c		7a		7b			7c		8a			8b...

STAR RATINGS and QUALIFIERS

A star rating is also included in the class rating to identify those "climbs of note" in the area. This system reflects the quality rather than the difficulty of a particular route and is perhaps the most subjective of the rating systems. Recognize that a quality rock for climbing has much to do with expectation and your feel for the rock. Climbers that have only experienced climbing on solid granite may feel uncomfortable with the feel of climbing on volcanic tuff until they have developed a feel for it. Quality ratings are often made in relation to a given area. This means a three-star route for an area with minimal rock quality may not compare well with a three-star route on a rock with excellent rock quality.

*   Enjoyable, recommended. Moves are often inconsistent in difficulty. May be dirty in places but rock quality is generally good.
**   Worth repeating. May have several unique moves worth storing into your memory banks.
***   Excellent route, the best the area has to offer. Good rock quality with fun moves that are fairly consistent in difficulty. May not offer a sense of exposure or a great view.
**** A great experience beyond making moves. Great exposure with a view, unique moves that are fairly consistent in difficulty.

Runout (R), Leader cannot fall (X), Toperope (TR), First Ascent (FA), First Toprope (FTR), Variation (Var.).

Dylan Ransom

ASHLAND BOULDERS

The Ashland Castles Bouldering Area is located on a steep hillside of rounded granitic boulders overlooking the town of Ashland. These unique boulders are nestled amongst a mystically beautiful and rare ninety-year-old growth Manzanita and Madrone. The area has been visited by climbers for at least thirty years. It is the largest source of boulder problems in the Rogue Valley. Known also as the Hitt Road Boulders, Strawberry Boulders, and Big Rock. The following boulder route information is not intended to be all-inclusive. It is provided as a guide to new climbers who are visiting the boulders for the first time.

The Ashland Castle boulders average 15 feet in height. The rock is sharp in places, loose in others. For the most part however, it is very solid. You will find everything from one-move wonders to highball cranking. Most boulder problems in the area range from 5.10-5.11 in difficulty. The boulder problems at Ashland Castles are rated with the V-scale, the standard grading system for most bouldering areas of the world. Problems graded V1 are pretty hard-in fact, the hardest problems on the hill are only V3 at this time. A person's size and experience with exposure while unroped, can have a significant influence on rating short boulder problems. The ratings given are only approximations and are offered to provide guidance.

Rogue

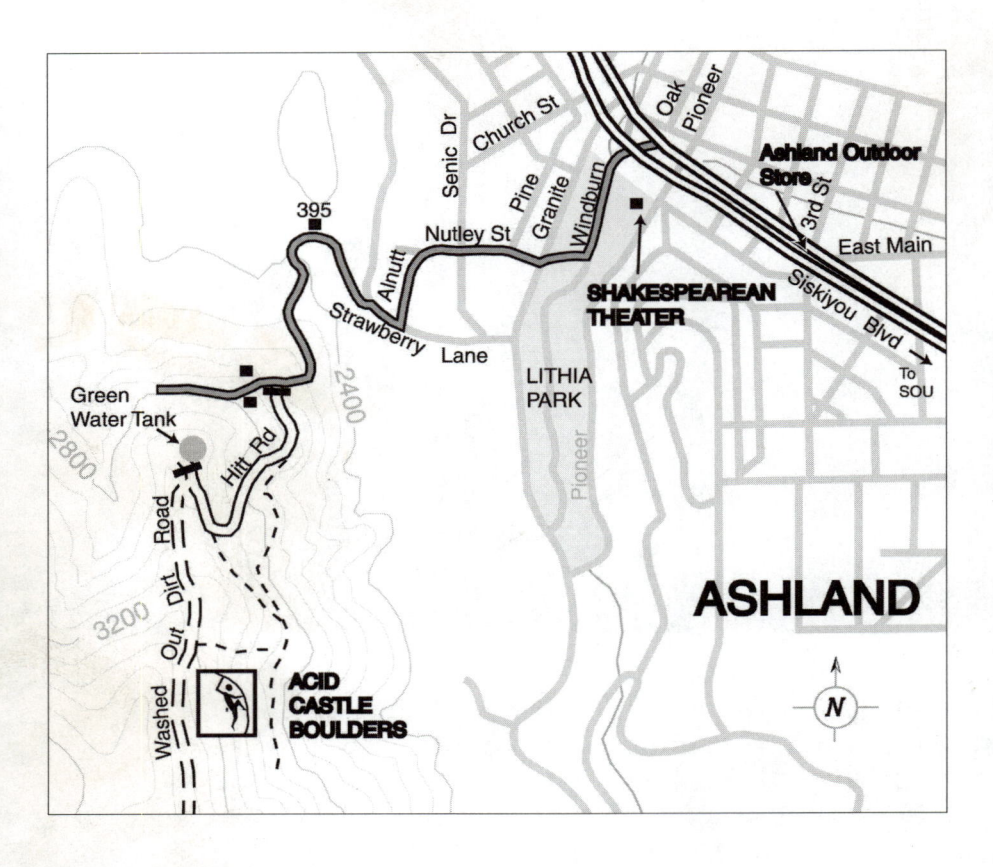

How To Get There

From Lithia Park in downtown Ashland, turn right onto Nutley Road. Nutley will turn from pavement to gravel. Continue up Nutley to Alnutt. Turn left onto Alnutt. Continue on Alnutt until it dead-ends into Strawberry Lane. Turn right up the steep hill onto Strawberry Lane. Strawberry climbs steeply, then makes a sharp switchback to the left. On the switchback turn, look for the driveway to 395 Strawberry on the right as an indicator that you are not lost. Hitt Road will be the first road to your left after 395 Strawberry. Hitt Road is a narrow-paved road blocked with a green metal gate. Beside this gate, there is a little red bus stop shed on the uphill side of the junction between Strawberry and Hitt. Use your own discretion about where to park, but don't block the gate. There are dirt pullouts to park in along Strawberry.

Upper Trail Access

Hitt Road ends at a large green water tank. Just before the water tank you will see a rutted dirt road climbing steeply up the left bank. Hike up this road. After a few minutes of hiking, you will come around a corner and see the top of your first boulder, about 20 feet downhill

Ashland Boulder

Overview Map

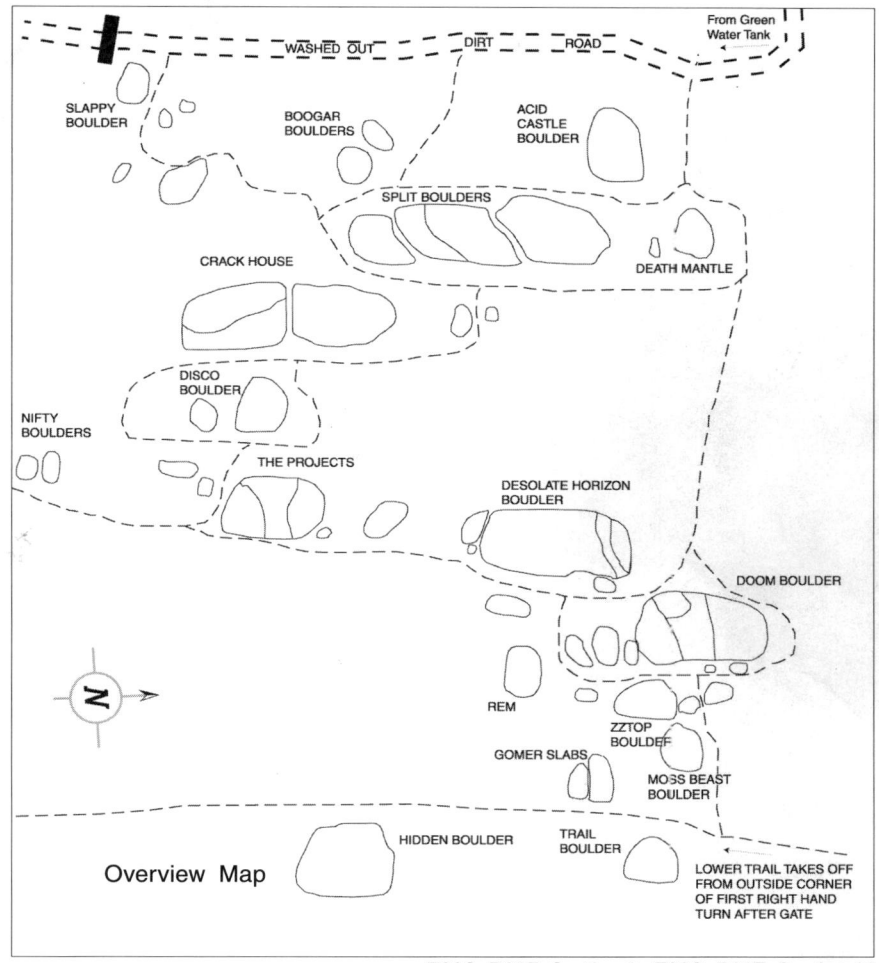

T38S, R01E, Section 8; T39S, R01E, Section 17

on your left. This tall boulder is the Ashland Castle, where you will find problem #54. Or, if you continue on the dirt road for a couple hundred feet, you will see, on the left, a small boulder with a little roof feature. This is the Slappy Boulder. Walk too far and you will come to a large berm across the road.

Ashland Boulder

LOWER TRAIL ACCESS

Hike up Hitt Road from the gate several hundred feet to the first right turn. On the outside of this turn, a trail leads off to the left (facing up-hill). The start of this trail first appears as a drainage ditch. This trail contours the slope to the lower boulders. At a little over halfway, you will jump a small ditch. Trail Boulder will be the first boulder visible on the left side of the trail, the rest of the lower boulders will be faintly visible on the right. Refer to the overview maps for navigation through the boulders.

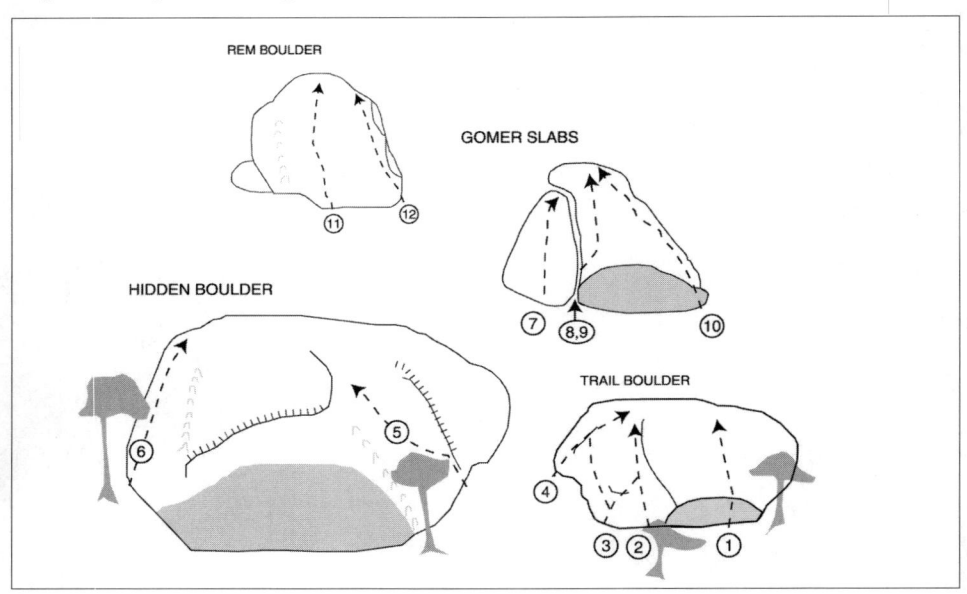

TRAIL BOULDER

1   Right side slab. Use tree root stuck to rock as foothold.
Trail Boulder Slab
* V0

2   Start atop tree trunk, up the seam on slopers.
Freudian Slip
* V0+

3   Start from big undercling left of tree trunk, finish up #2.
Low Start
** V2

4 Poison V0+ — To the left is a very short problem up a seam. Ground slopes heavily, so start is weird.

Hidden Boulder

5 Intro Crack V2 — The low-angle crack.

6 Unnamed V2 — The far left side of the boulder, up a groove.

Gomer Slabs

7 Deception * V0+ — Contrived immediately left of the crack, using sharp pockets. Trickier than it looks.

8 Crack For The Masses * V2 — The great, but short lieback. V1 sit-down-start.

9 Tiny Dancer * V2 — Make one move up #8, move right onto thin face.

10 Bottom Feeder V1 — Far right side sit-down-start on square jug. Throw left to good hold and walk up the slab.

REM Boulder

11
REM
*** V2

Takes a stellar line up the thin face on small edges. Funky topout.

12
Flakes
V2

Easy flakes on right side.

ZZTop and Moss Beast Boulders

13
Unnamed
V1

Right edge of short, squarish boulder. Sit-down-start on jug to hard mantle.

14
Unnamed
V2

Balancey moves on right side of low-angle face. Scary.

15
Wailing Soul
* V1

Start with a high left side-pull, and high right in-cut. Throw left and finish up #14.

16
Alcove
V0+

Start in alcove, grovel right and top out.

17
Leapyear
* V0

Start with left side-pull/under-cling, leap to the sloping lip, and press it out. Fun.

18
Static
* V0+

Start just right on small edges. Tricky balance moves.

Ashland Boulder 55

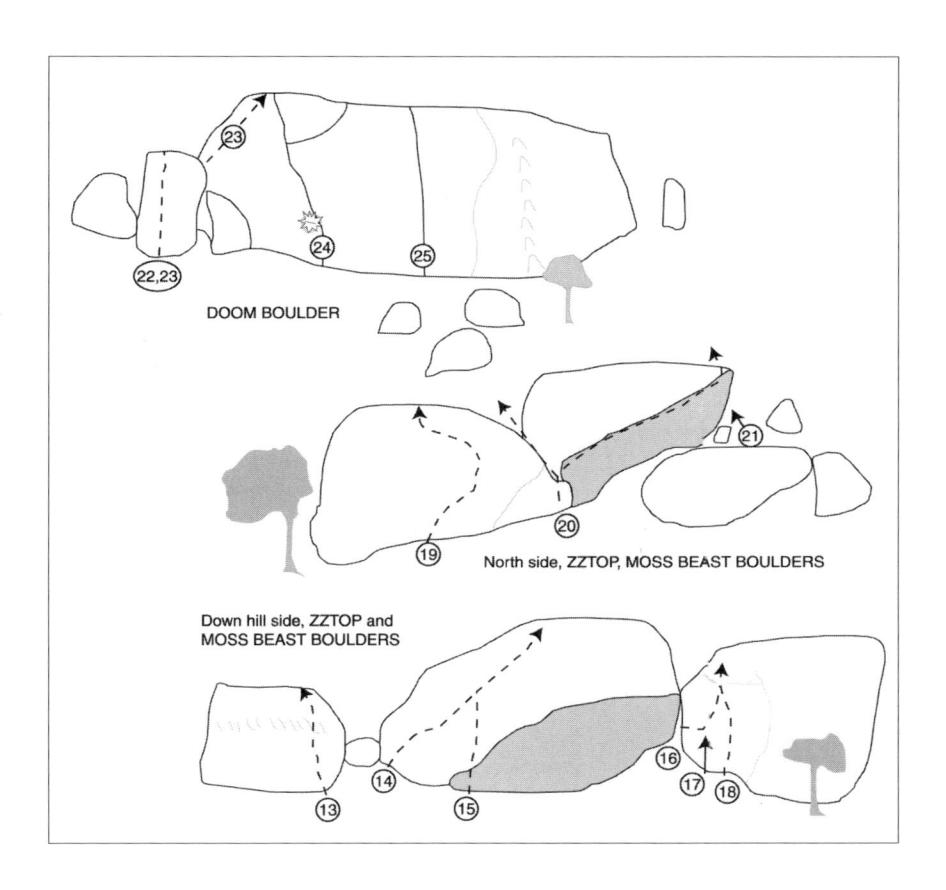

DOOM BOULDER

North side, ZZTOP, MOSS BEAST BOULDERS

Down hill side, ZZTOP and MOSS BEAST BOULDERS

19   Start on the steep face, move feet right to ramp reaching for a sloping
Joe's Problem   lip. Reachy.
* V3

20   Sit-down-start on left side of boulder. Traverse lip to right, mantle at
ZZTop   arete. Great warmup.
** V2

21   Sit-down-start to steep arete. Short problem with great, tricky moves.
The Laying On Of   A great variation starts standing with your left hand on the arete holds,
Hands   and the right on the sloping lip. Move right and top-out.
* V3

Rogue

Doom Boulder

22 Ashen Ghoul ** V1
Sweet double arete. So-so landing, but great moves.

23 Unnamed V2
Scary face above Ashen Ghoul, but quite easy.

24 Got Wood * V0
Wide highball crack. Uses knobs on a small tree in the crack. Sit-down-start same grade.

25 Crack Of Doom *** V2
Bad name, great route! Bring gear to toprope, aid, or lead.

Nifty Boulders

26 Unnamed V0
Left boulder. Start hanging on low jug, pull up, and mantle. Fun.

27 Fornication * V1
Right boulder. Go to jug at lip, and pull very difficult mantle.

28 Staircase V0
Silly problem right next to wooden ladder. One move, but pretty good.

Ashland Boulder

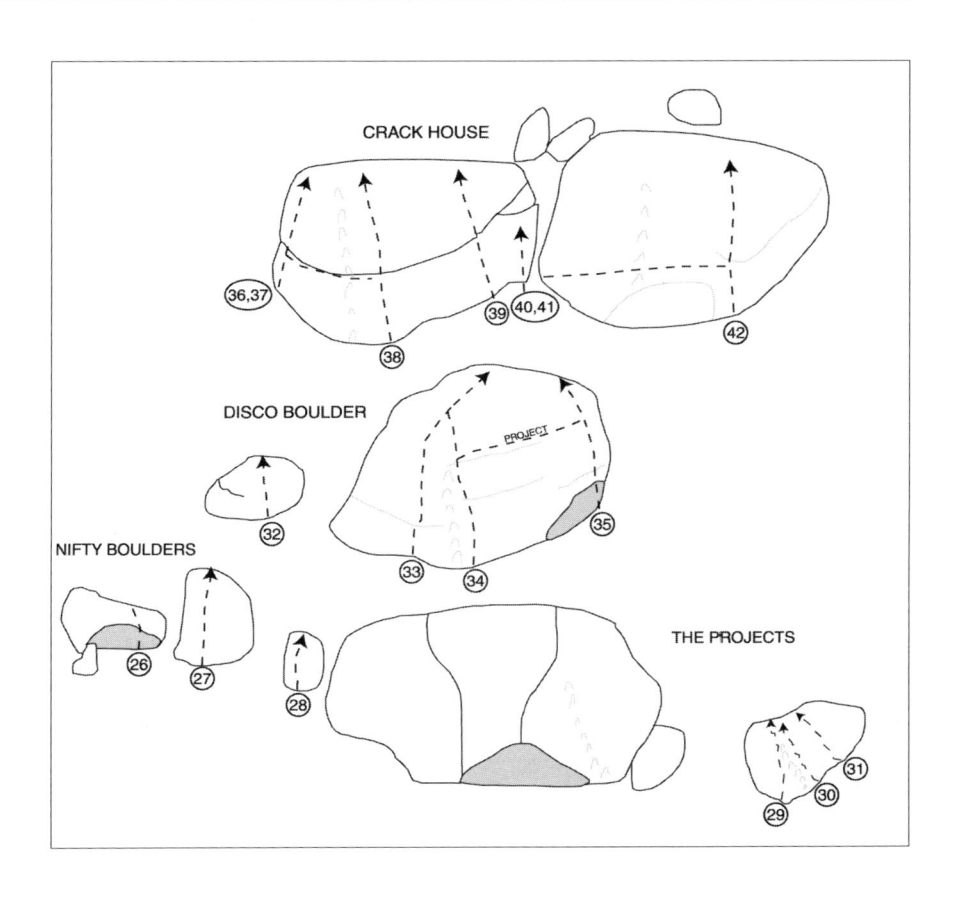

29 Shoot The Messinger V1 — Climb downhill face using the right arete. Fun moves.

30 Waco V0 — Climb the left side of the slab using the nice dish.

31 Limber V2 — Climb blank slab just to the right.

Rogue

Disco Boulder

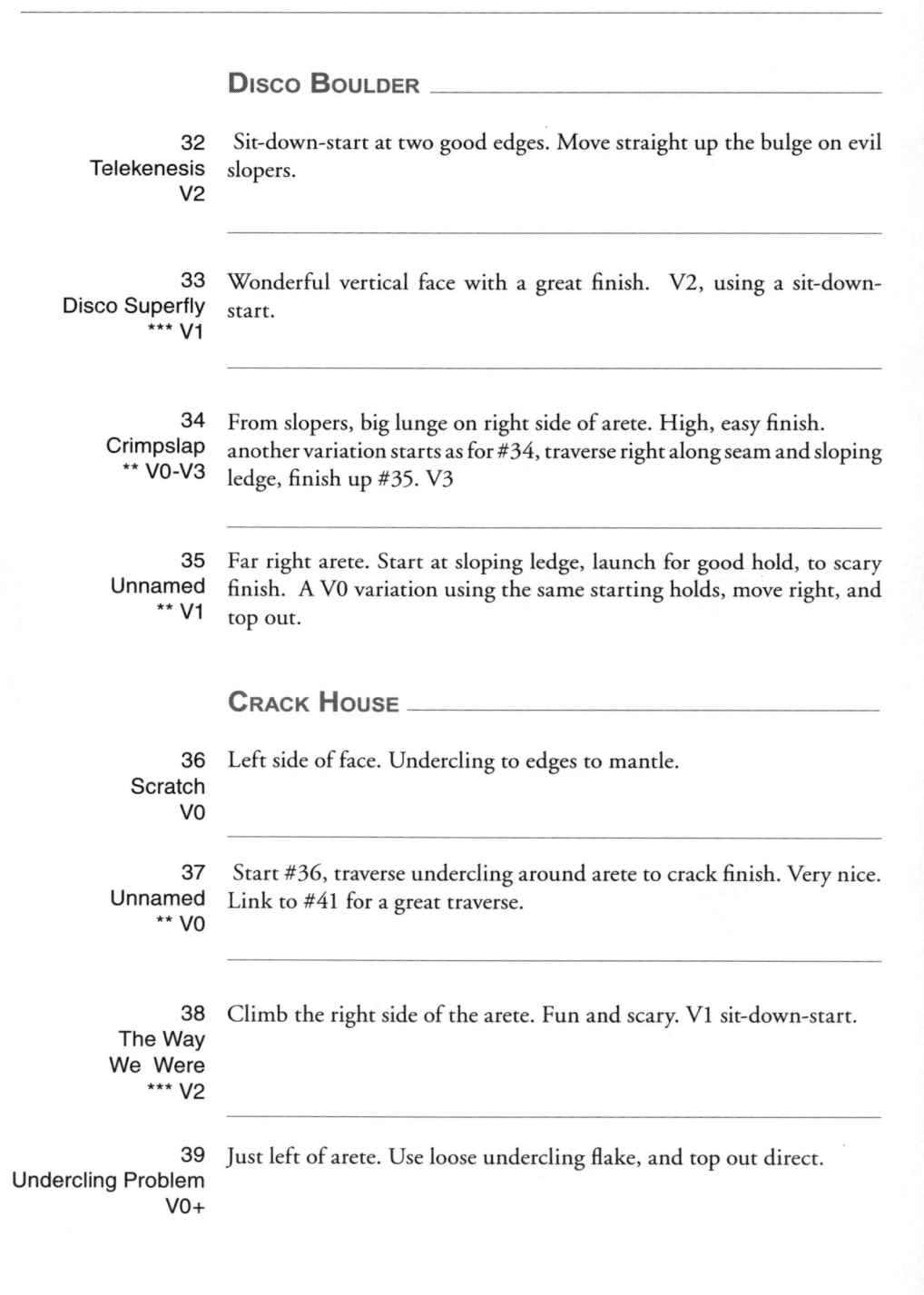

32 Telekenesis V2 — Sit-down-start at two good edges. Move straight up the bulge on evil slopers.

33 Disco Superfly * V1** — Wonderful vertical face with a great finish. V2, using a sit-down-start.

34 Crimpslap ** V0-V3 — From slopers, big lunge on right side of arete. High, easy finish. another variation starts as for #34, traverse right along seam and sloping ledge, finish up #35. V3

35 Unnamed ** V1 — Far right arete. Start at sloping ledge, launch for good hold, to scary finish. A V0 variation using the same starting holds, move right, and top out.

Crack House

36 Scratch V0 — Left side of face. Undercling to edges to mantle.

37 Unnamed ** V0 — Start #36, traverse undercling around arete to crack finish. Very nice. Link to #41 for a great traverse.

38 The Way We Were * V2** — Climb the right side of the arete. Fun and scary. V1 sit-down-start.

39 Undercling Problem V0+ — Just left of arete. Use loose undercling flake, and top out direct.

40 Basic V2		Climb the arete/chimney.
41 Wake Up The Monkey ** V2		Start between the boulders, go right, finish up #42. Refer to description for route #42.
42 Double Mantle ** V1		Heelhook onto huge jug, and pull two sweet mantles. Scary. Note: the jug has become very loose, use discretion.

SPLIT BOULDERS

43 World's Sexiest Offwidth *** V0+		The obvious lieback, with strange crux at top. Classic!
44 A Special Place In Hell For People Like You V2		Climb as a squeeze chimney, top out with armbars.
45 Unnamed * V1 w/ V3 var		From atop flat boulder, move up to loose flake and top out. Scary landing.
46 Bloodbath ** V1		Classic lieback/offwidth crack. Sloping and technical. V2 sit-down-start. A V3 variation is to start from the left, with hands on jugs at the base of the crack. Move right and finish up #46.

Ashland Boulder

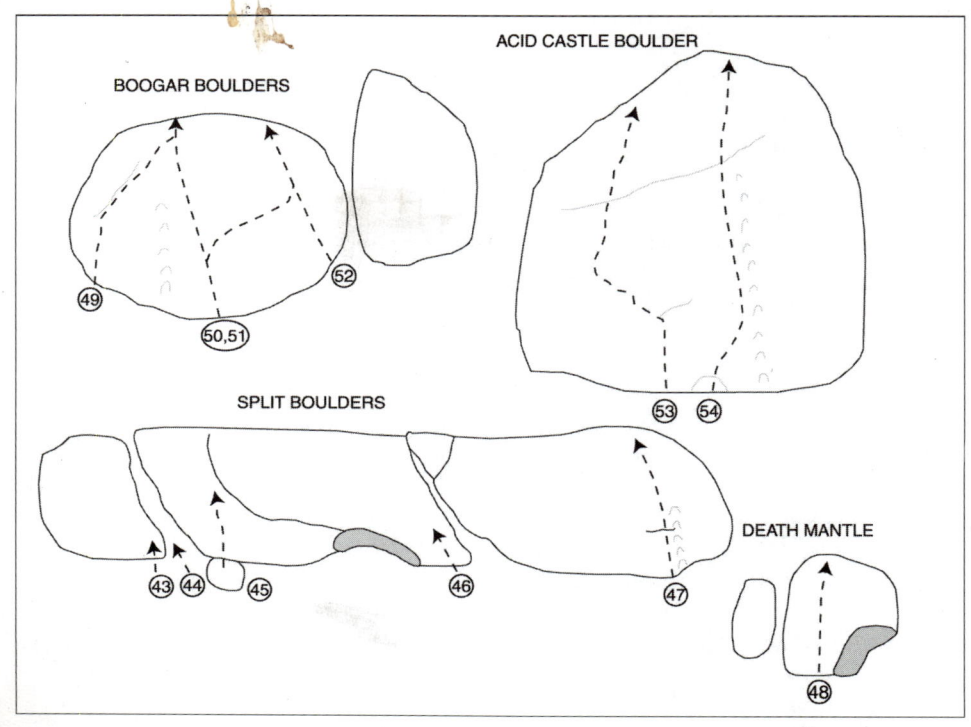

	47 Just Less Dope V2	Low start on a big sloper. Lunge left to lip, and top out. V0+ stand up start.

	48 Death Mantle ** V1	Sit-down-start on jugs, up to more jugs and tricky topout. Not scary like the name implies.

Boogar Boulders

	49 Seamin' V1	Start with left side in seam, and right side on whatever works, and pull a hard move.

	50 Gammy's Gettin' Upset * V2	The thin left side of the wall. Tricky footwork problem.

Ashland Boulder

51 Traverse V1 — Start as for #50, but move right to finish up #52.

52 The Fall Of Boogar V0 — The right side of the face. Delicate moves.

Ashland Castle Boulder

53 Unnamed * V2 — Start on flexing flake, stem left, and move up the thin face. Bad landing.

54 Castle In The Sky **** V3 — The arete. Sustained and super-classic. Injury potential if you don't toprope.

Slappy Boulder

55 Unnamed V0 — Climb on left side. Thin mantle move.

56 Slabby Galore * V0+ — The middle of the thin face. Suprisingly hard.

57 Mr. Chainsaw * V0+ — The arete. Tricky topout, bad landing.

58 Unnamed V0+ — Traverse square boulder from left to right, around arete, and mantle.

62 Ashland Boulder

SLAPPY BOULDER
Uphill Face

SLAPPY BOULDER, Downhill face

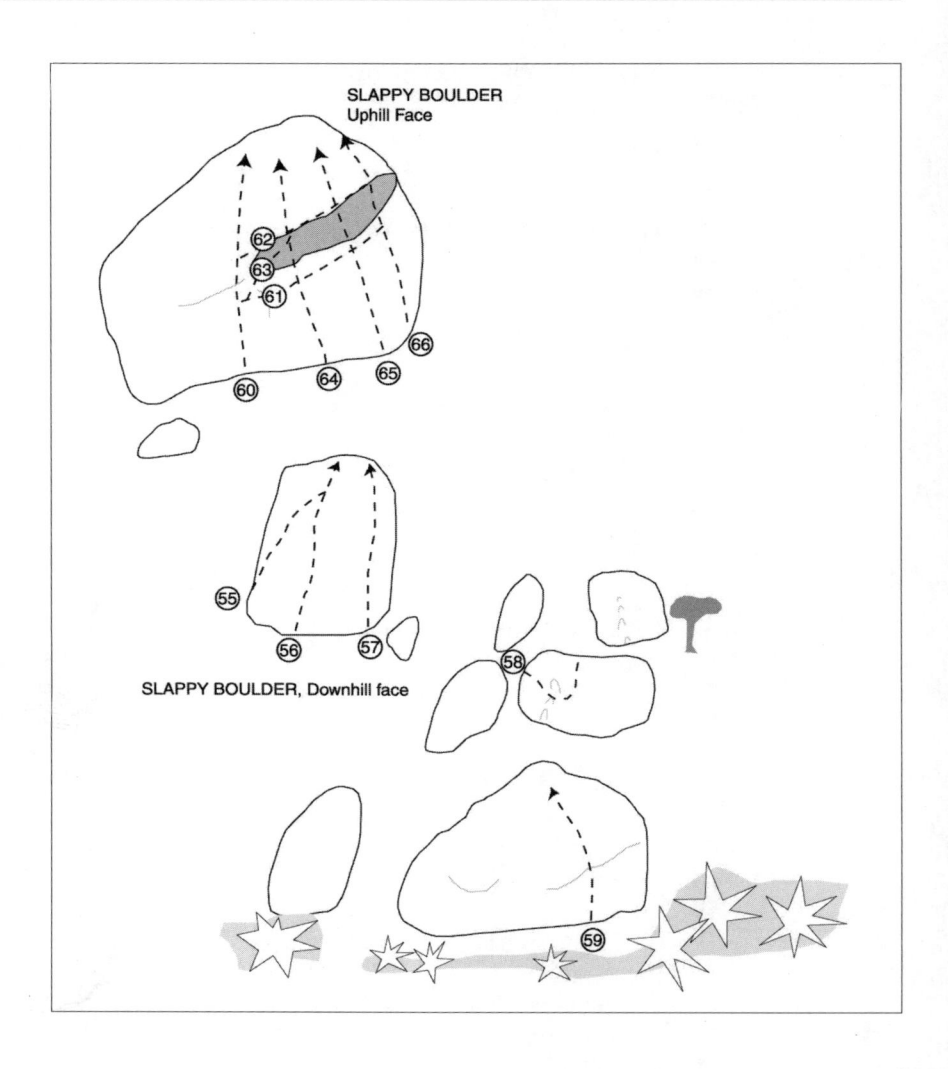

59 Hidden in the bushes. Climb straight up using ramp and shallow pockets. Stay left.
Unnamed
V0+

60 Start at a left crimper and right jug, throw to sloping dishes. Sweet.
Slappy Gilmore
** V0+

61	Wax	Start as for #60, traverse right under roof to finish on #66. Tricky moves.
	V1	

| 62 | Unnamed | Do first move of #60, traverse lip to the right to finish up #66. |
| | V0+ | |

| 63 | Contrive This | Start as for #60, lunge up and right to flat edge. |
| | V1 | |

| 64 | Unnamed | Start under roof, reach to flat edge, and top out. |
| | V0 | |

| 65 | Unnamed | Start under roof, reach to some tiny slopers at lip, and top out. |
| | V0+ | |

| 66 | Unnamed | Uncontrived mantle on right side of boulder. |
| | V2 | |

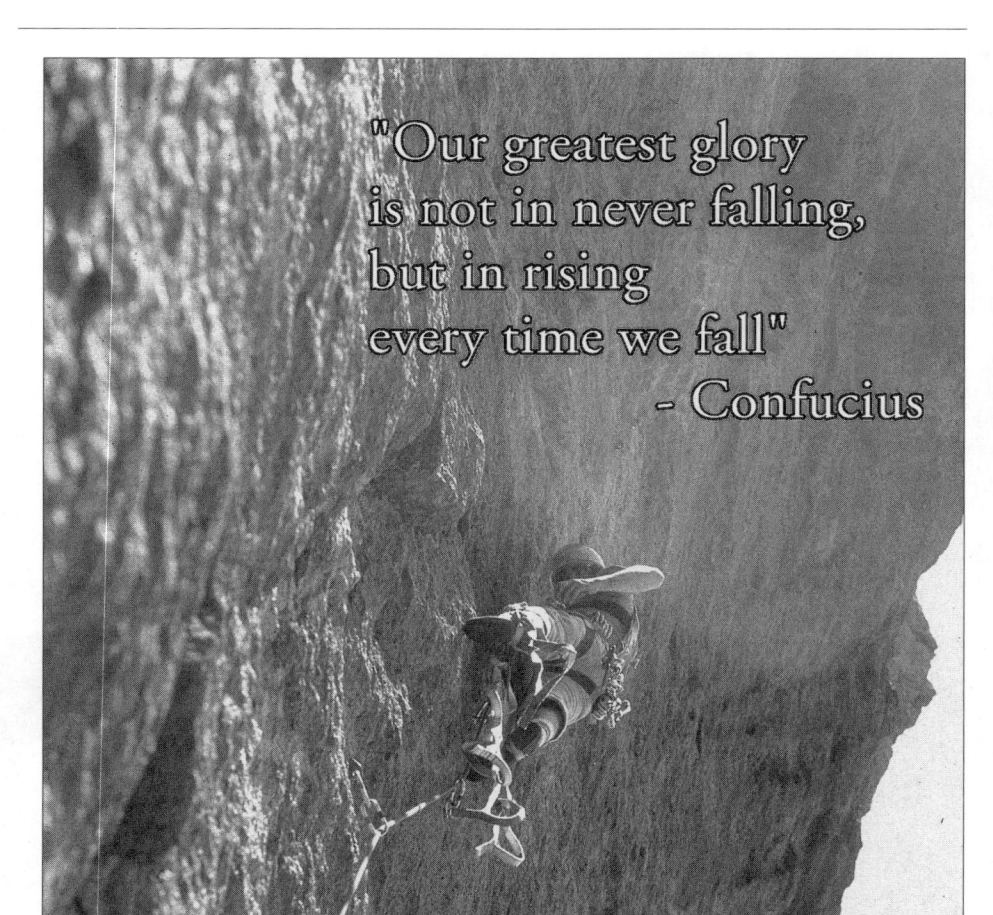

> "Our greatest glory is not in never falling, but in rising every time we fall"
> — Confucius

Photo: Greg Orton

By Jerry Messinger and Jim Davis.

Only 30 to 45 minutes out of Ashland, Mount Ashland offers climbers a secluded high elevation experience on top of the Siskiyou Mountains. Most years the snow is melted enough for climbing in late May. At 7500 feet, climbing can be cool even in midsummer. The rock at Mount Ashland is granitic (diorite). Several short cracks and dihedrals exist. They are easily protected with a standard rack, usually no wider than three inches.

Climbs range from 20 to 70 feet high. Although more suited as a toprope and bouldering area, there is some potential for new route developement in the future. Currently there are 16 established routes on Mount Ashland. They range from 5.2 to 5.11c. in difficulty. Seventy percent of these routes are 5.10a or less. All top anchors can be reached by scrambling to the top and walk-offs are usually third class or simple fourth class. Loose rock, scree, and gravel can make getting to and off the top of many of these routes tricky, if not dangerous.

Rogue

Mt. Ashland

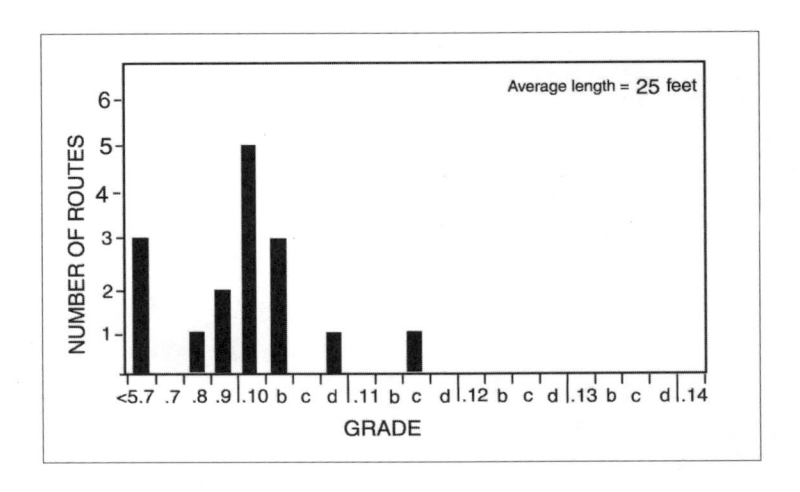

How To Get There

To reach the climbing area at Mount Ashland, drive past the lodge and continue up through the upper parking lot and onto Forest Service Road 20. Continue on FS-20 taking your first right onto FS-300. Take FS-300 to the top of Mount Ashland. Park in the small lot on top about 50 feet below the large round radar station.

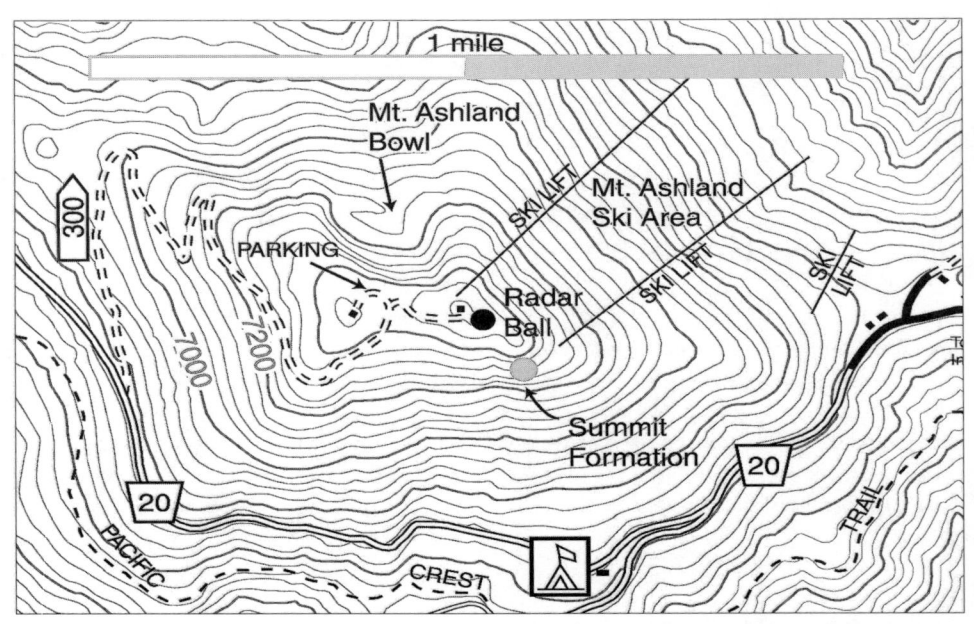

T20S, R01E, Section 21 Ashland Ranger District, Rogue River National Forest

The Summit Formation

can be located by walking south along the ridge top from the radar ball. Contour right, around the base of the large outcrop located at the end of the ridge. FA Dan Higgins, 1989.

| 1 | Opie & Andie | Crux before first bolt. | 5.10b*** |
| 2 | Snowbind | | 5.5** |

Mt. Ashland Bowl

Northwest from this parking area is the second chute of the Mount Ashland ski bowl. Further left is the third chute.

3	Graffiti Rock	5.6-5.9
4	Green M&M's	5.11c (TR)
5	Late Again	5.9***
6	Anita Hill Memorial Whiners Climb	5.10a (TR)
7	Long Dong Silver	5.10a (TR)
8	Crack	NR**
9	Amp Chimney	5.2
10	Board Head	5.8***
11	Fishhooks on the whip	5.10b***
12	Dihedral	5.7
13	Black Slab Left	NR
14	Black Slab Right	NR
15	White Slab Crack	5.7**
16	White Slab Left	5.10b***
17	White Slab Right	5.10d
18	Dihedral/Arete to face	5.10a

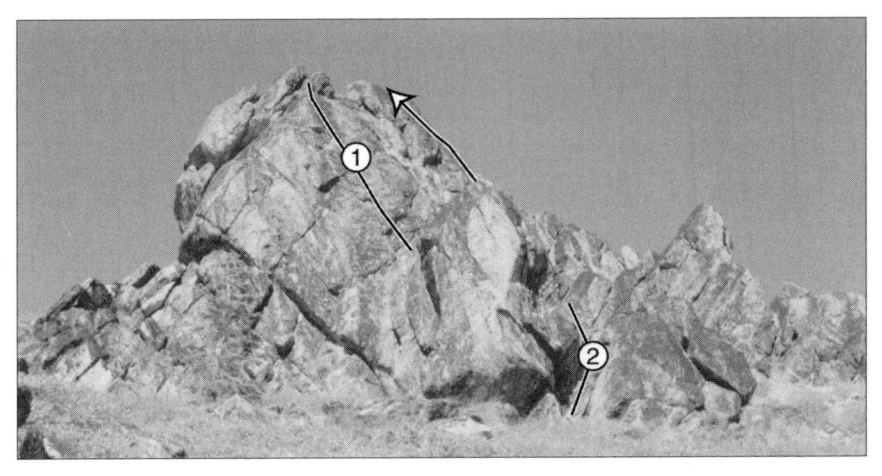

68　Mt. Ashland

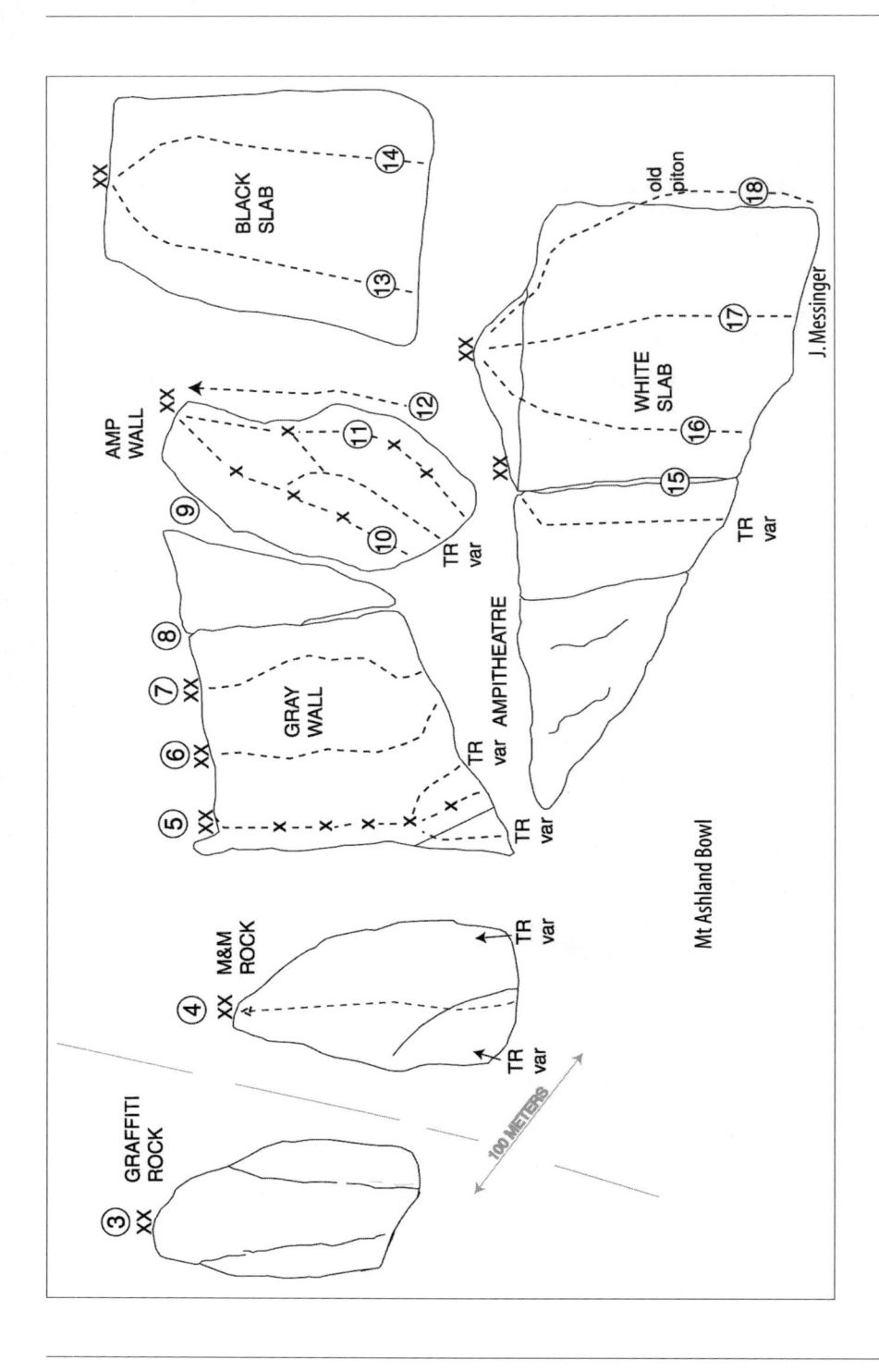

Route s descriptions by Jerry Messinger and Jim Davis

The sandstone that surrounds Emigrant Lake originally formed as a nonmarine outwash plain that was later faulted and possibly altered by hot fluids percolating through the fault zone. The rock units here vary from layers of medium grain volcanic sandstone to pebbly sandstone tilting to the southeast. Located at just over 2,000 feet elevation with a southwest aspect, this rock offers year-round climbing. Routes are 30 to 80 feet high. They are easily accessed from the top and offer an ideal place for toproping. Most of the routes are bolted for lead with a few requiring gear placements. Poison oak is present, but can be avoided by using care and staying on trails.

70   Emigrant Lake

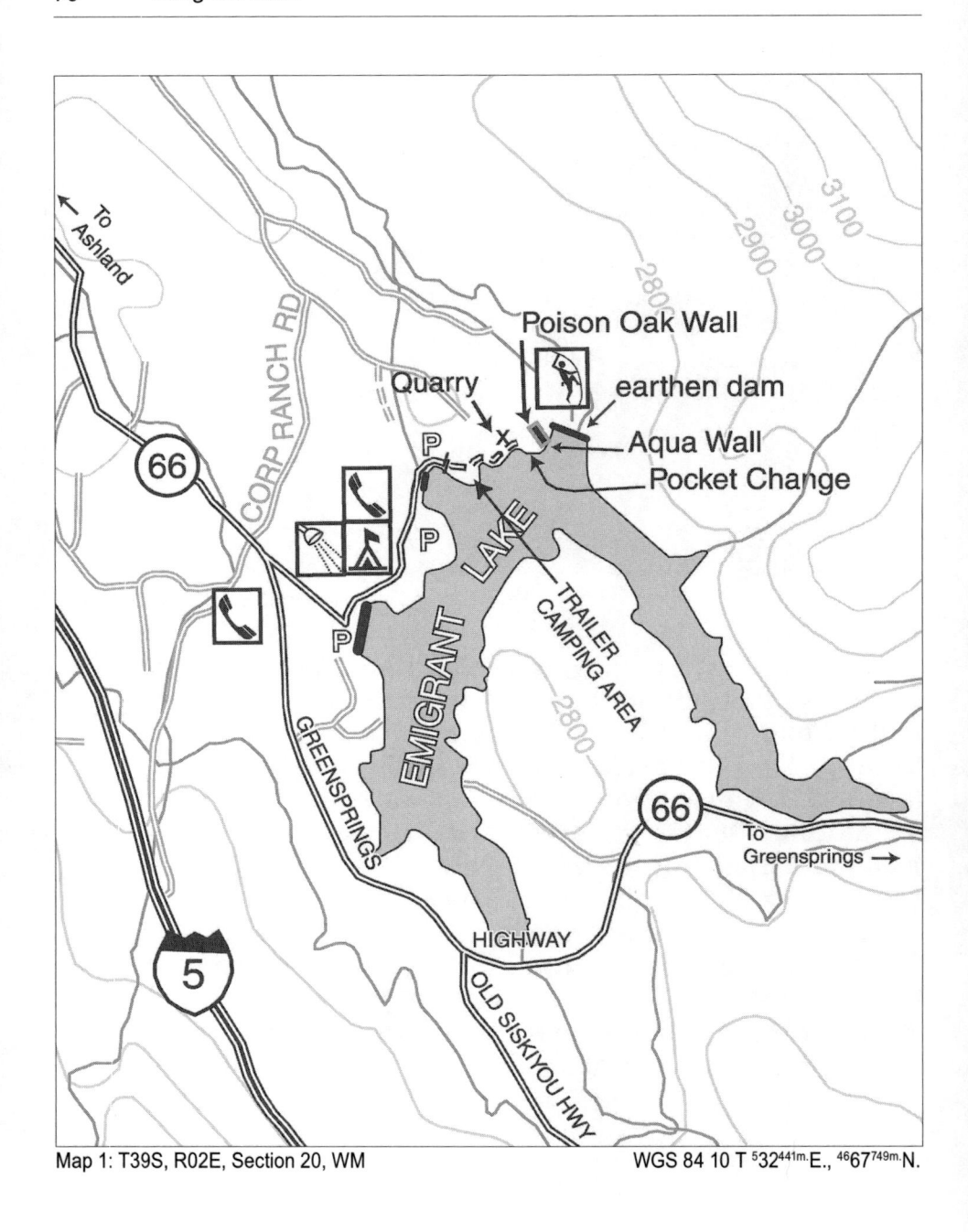

How to Get There
From Interstate 5, take the Ashland Exit 14. Turn east onto Green Springs Road (Highway 66). Stay on Green Springs Road for 3 miles to Emigrant Lake.

Turn east at the main entrance to Emigrant Lake. Proceed through the gate at the top of the dike and on to the pay station managed by Jackson County Parks and Recreation (current fee is $3.00). Follow the road to the far end of the park and across a small spillway. Park near the end of the road between the spillway and entrance to the trailer camping area. Proceed on foot on the upper paved road through the trailer camp to a dirt road. Follow the dirt road east around the lake's edge until it terminates at the lake shore, just past a small quarry. From here follow a steep trail up the left embankment, then right along the top of the cliff following the lake's edge. (Note: there are trails above this, but they have more poison oak on them.) When the trail forks, take the lower trail to the right, which leads to Poison Oak and Aqua Walls. Note: Just past Poison Oak Wall and Aqua Wall will be an earthen dam.

Route Descriptions
Emigrant's Poison Oak Wall dries quickly and usually remains climbable throughout the year. Climbs here are short, ranging from 30 to 80 feet in length. Three fourths of the routes on the Poison Oak Wall are rated below 5.10a. All routes are easily toproped. The Aqua Wall has over hangs and thin friction climbing making it a much more challenging area to climb. Over half the climbs on the Aqua Wall are rated 5.11c or more. During most years, Aqua Wall remains partially submerged between March and July.

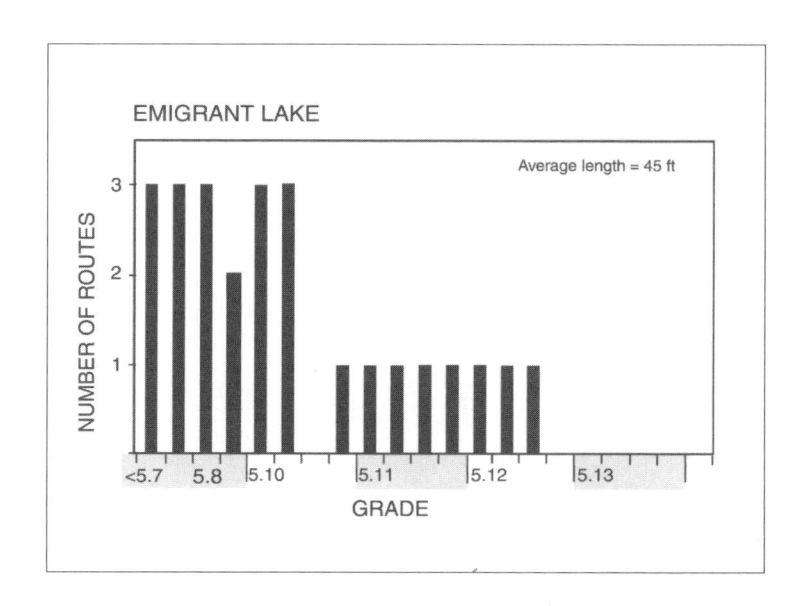

Emigrant Lake

Poison Oak Wall
(Topo A)
Many of these routes have probably been climbed, soloed, lead, and toproped for years. Little information is available on first ascents.

1 Back Bonker Arete ***5.11c** — Located on left side of the gully on far left end of Poison Oak Wall. Tricky steep moves on very good rock. Belayer and spotter recommended. 2 bolts.

2 Buttmunch **5.10/ 5.11** — Located on left side of gully, just right of *Back Bonker Arete*. Can be lead on gear, but is mainly a top rope or solo problem, with traverse entry possible.

3 Hippie Teacher **5.4** — Low angle on bottom, becomes steeper on top. Friction with horizontal cracks.

4 Fire! **5.5** — Thin crack. Pockets and horizontal cracks. Gear placements.

5 Mr. Anderson **5.6** — Another good learning route or warm up.

6 Tool Shed **5.3** — Obvious sloping ramp with bouldery cracks. Gear placement. Watch for loose blocks.

Jim Shannan (right) rappelling from the top of Other Kids (5.10d); Sean Bagshaw climbing the top block of Cornholio (5.10a). Greg Orton

Rogue

74 Emigrant Lake

7 Bug Off ***5.8	Has TR variations left (5.6/5.7), and right (5.7). FA Jim Davis and Steve Johnson, 1989.
8 Beavis **5.7	Starts to left of *Butthead* and merges with *Butthead* at the third bolt. A great, clean line with neat holds, especially near the start.
9 Butthead **5.8	Good rock and some interesting moves. A warm-up for harder climbs. FA Jerry Messinger, Jim Davis.
10 Cornholio ***5.10a	Excellent moves with an exciting finish. Stay on the line without climbing off to either side or climbing the left crack. The top has a 5.6 finish. Note that the 10a rating is for the direct finish. FA Jim Davis, Jerry Messinger.
11 Other Kids **5.10d	Roof problem with two cruxes. Both the start and upper roof problems are tricky. Caution: Do not miss clipping into the fourth bolt. FA Jerry Messinger.

December climbing on Emigrant Lake sandstone. Christine Dianni climbs *Bug-Off* (5.7). Greg Orton

Emigrant Lake

This clip off route

15b 15c 16

Topo B1: John Asay, moving left over the roof onto Ren (5.10b). Greg Orton

REN WALL
(Topo A, B1, B2, C)
Ren Wall is in the middle section of the formation between The Poison Oak Wall and Aqua Wall. The Ren Wall area is most easily recognized by the white droppings that stain the rock below a small cave.

12
Bus Ride
AKA Ritalin Child
**5.10a
Starts 25 feet uphill from *Burritos*. A face climb that ends on the catwalk to the top of the wall. Easier if you veer off to the sides. Approx. 3 bolts. FA Jerry Messinger, 2001.

13
Burritos
***5.8
Starts 15 feet to the left of *Nachos*. Good face climbing to the little roof above. 4 bolts.
FA Jerry Messinger, 2001.

14a
Nachos - The Jim Davis Memorial Route
**5.7
Starts 5 to 10 feet left of *Ren*, *Stimpy*, and *Wimpy*. Climb up under the black alcove. 3 bolts. FA Jerry Messinger, 2001.

14b
Spaghetti variation
**5.10a
A variation between *Nachos* and *Burritos*. Same start as *Nachos*. At second bolt break left and tackle the steep nose straight on. Reach for the jug. Clip the third bolt on *Nachos* to your right. FA Jerry Messinger, 2001.

15a
Wimpy
****5.7
Common start with *Ren* and *Stimpy*. Climb past 5 bolts to the first set of chain anchors. A fun route.
FA Jim Davis, 1991.

Mandy Bucey (age 10) climbing to the left of *Bugoff* (5.6).
Greg Orton

Emigrant Lake

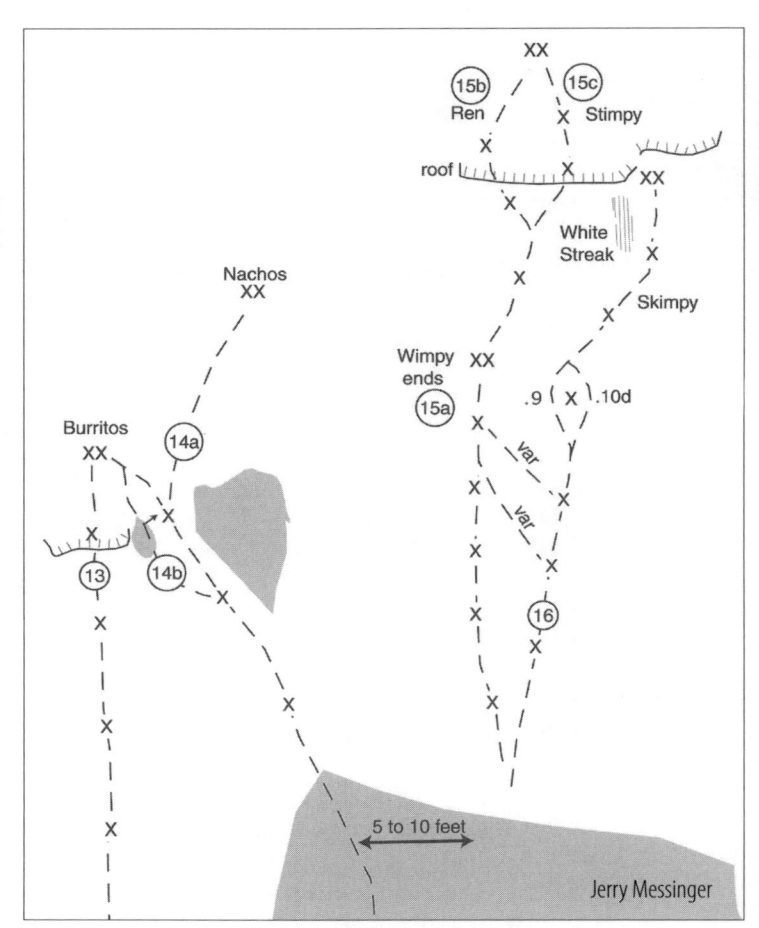

Ren Wall Topo B2

15b Ren **5.10b	Common start with *Stimpy* and *Wimpy*. Climb past 5 bolts, the chain anchor, and head for the roof above. At the roof clip the left bolt, climb left, then up and over. Shares top anchors with *Stimpy*. FA Jim Davis, 1991.
15c Stimpy ****5.11a/b	Common start with *Ren* and *Wimpy*. As with *Ren* climb past the same 5 bolts, the chain anchor, and head for the roof above. Climb the roof up and over without veering to the right. Once on top the roof continue up the fall line to the top anchors shared with *Ren*. The roof is reminiscent of a Gunk's roof. FA Jerry Messinger, 1991.

Emigrant Lake 79

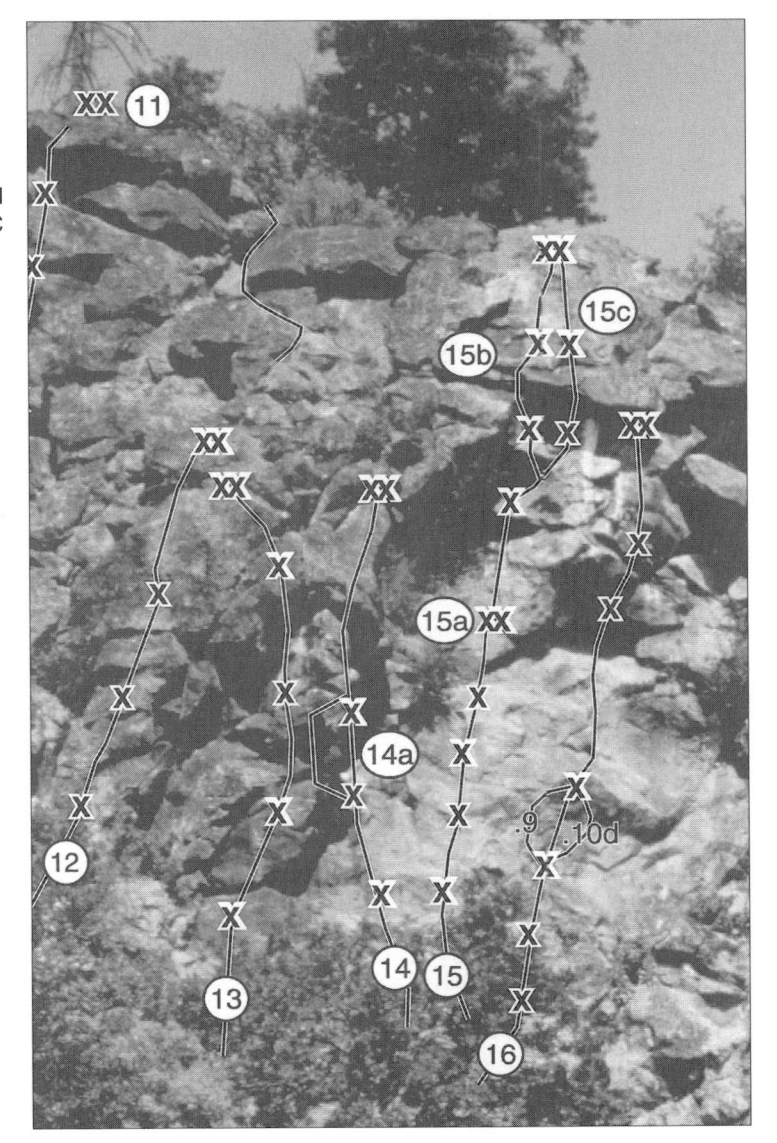

Ren Wall
Topo C

16 Skimpy ***5.10d w/ 5.9 var
Start just right of *Wimpy-Ren-Stimpy* climbing the easy ramp, then around the bulge left (5.9), or right (5.10d), and then up to some intimidating bulges that have fun and surprisingly positive jugs. FA Jerry Messinger, 2001.

Note: an alternative variation is to continue left from *Skimpy* and top out at the first set of chain anchors on *Wimpy*.

Rogue

Aqua Wall and Aqua Cave
(Topos E and F)

This area is often submerged between March and July when the lake level is up. Most of these routes were the efforts of Jerry Messinger with Jim Davis during the 1990s, with Dan Higgins and Nathan Kerr making significant contributions.

**17
Pet Semitary
5.8
One of the longer routes at Emigrant. Mostly bolts but a nut or cam is needed above the first bolt. 4 bolts and gear placements to 1 inch. The upper rock sounds hollow and potentially loose. FA Jim Davis, 1997.

**18
Beyond the Siskiyou Sky
5.10a
Another longer route for Emigrant, with some nice roof moves at the end. Some gear placements. FA Jerry Messinger, 1997.

**19
TR variations
5.11/5.12
Hard moves on a bulging seam.

**20
Devastator
***5.12a**
Steep wall with long moves. Pulling over the final lip is the crux. FA Jerry Messinger, 1991.

**21
Reefer Finish
5.12b
Devastator to *Gloo*. At the lip, do hard moves to join Gloo. Finish on *Gloo*. FA Nathan Kerr, 1993.

**22
Full Link Up
****5.12c**
Devastator to Sniff. The hardest route in Southern Oregon for several years was the *Devastator* linked with *Gloo*, and finishing on *Sniff*. FA Jerry Messinger, 1994.

**23
Gloo
***11c**
Climb the steep jugs. Pull left over the nose and then work straight up to the belay anchors after fourth bolt. Note that the fourth bolt is used for *Sniff* and is not part of the original *Gloo* route. *Gloo* follows the weakness to the top. A variation finishes up the prow with *Sniff*. FA Dan Higgins, 1990.

> "When choosing between two evils, I always like to try the one I've never tried before."
> —Mae West

Joe Chaves climbing Devastator on Aqra Wall. Jerry Messinger

82 Emigrant Lake

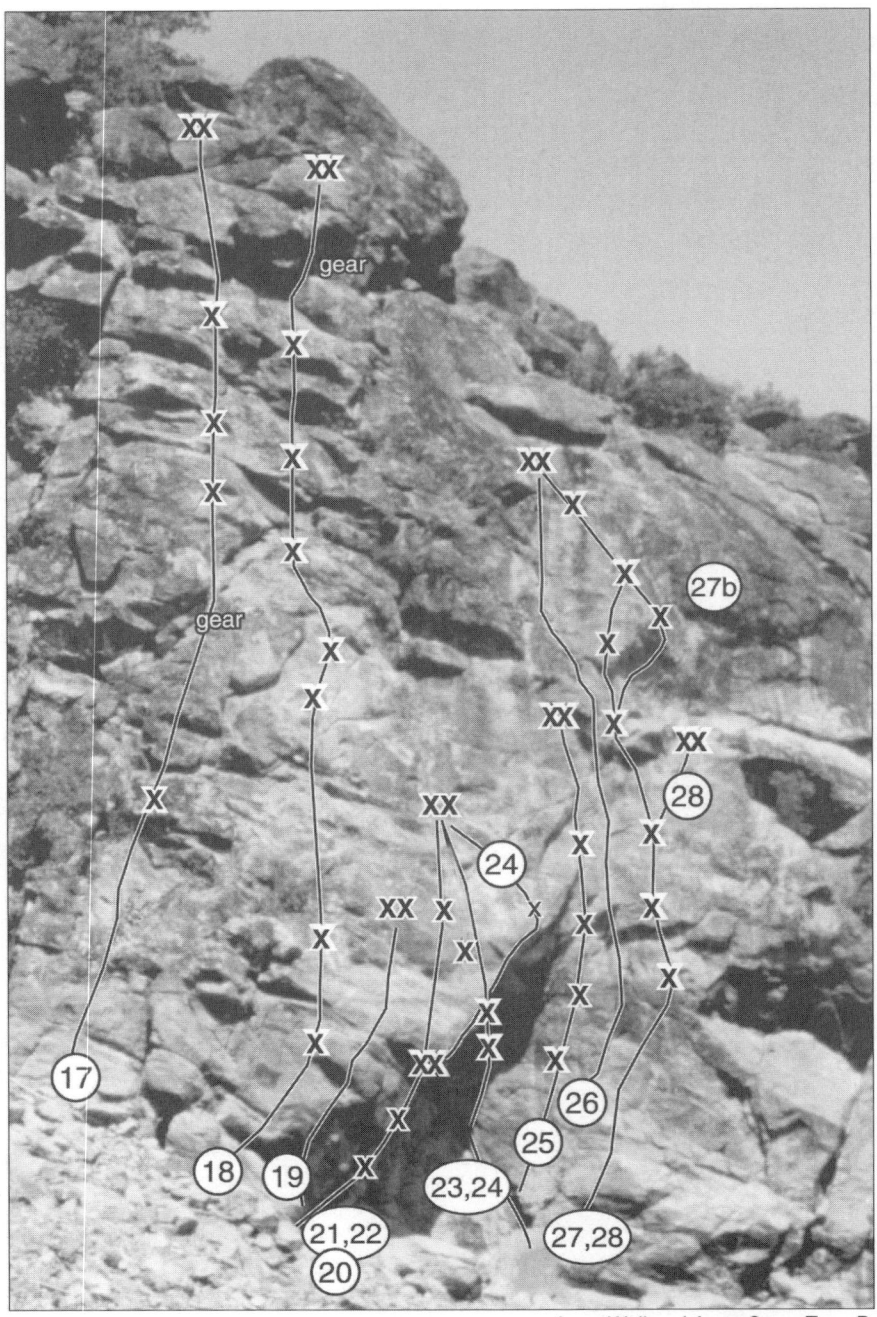

Aqua Wall and Aqua Cave, Topo D

Emigrant Lake 83

Aqua Cave
Topo E

24 Sniff ****5.11d
Finish up right, edge of arete. It is assumed you do not go left on the *Gloo* ledge before the finish, which is a rest and lowers the grade. Stay on the arete of the overhang. A little contrived perhaps, but not really once you do it. 5 bolts, sharing common top anchors with *Gloo*.
FA Jerry Messinger, 1991.

25 Capt. Horatio Horn Blower *** 5.11c
Single bouldery crux; stay on route. Good, clean rock.
FA Jerry Messinger, September 1990; Prep Dan Higgins.

Rogue

Jerry Messinger bouldering on Beavis (5.8).
Greg Orton

26
Poison Oak Crack
**5.7

Nice line, but watch out for poison oak. Easily toproped from Aquaman anchor. Requires gear to 1 inch. FA Jim Davis.

27a
Aqua Man
****5.10b

Climb through a technical crux at the second bolt, then hang on for the upper bulge which is taken slightly to the left. There are great natural pockets. FA Jim Davis.

27b
Hard Man
**5.11+

This is a one-bolt variation from the fourth bolt of Aqua Man slightly right to climb the upper bulge straight on. FA Jerry Messinger, 1997.

28
Aqua Weenie
**5.10a

First 3 bolts of Aqua Man. Avoid the 5.10b roof above by turning right and rapping from lower anchor. FA Jim Davis.

29
Pocket Change
**5.8

Follow the lakeshore back towards the recreation park to the next rock outcropping from the Aqua Wall (refer to Map 1). Pocket Change is a short slab climb near the beach. 30 feet with 3 bolts. This route is often covered by water. Check the bolts before leading it. FA Dan Higgins, 1989.

GREENSPRINGS

Jerry Messinger and Joe Chavez

Greensprings currently has approximately thirty-three established routes that range from 5.5 to 5.12b. The basalt columns of Greensprings range to 90 feet in height. The top of the columns is easily accessed, but require care due to loose scree on top. Some routes require long slings when establishing topropes. Greensprings Butte is on private property with the landowner enjoying his privacy on top. Limiting your activity to the lower walls only and cleaning up after yourself and others, will help to insure the access we currently enjoy. Area hazards are light poison oak and many of the top anchors that require experience to establish topropes.

Three guides have been written over the past ten years recording the history of climbing the Greensprings formation. The first of these was Rock Climbing in Southern Oregon, 1991, by Jerry Messinger, the second A Climber's Guide to Emigrant Lake and The Greensprings, by Chris Elder, and the most recent was A Climber's Guide to the Greensprings Climbing Area, 1995, by Mahlon Kerr-Valentic. Crack ratings are based on staying in the crack.

Greensprings

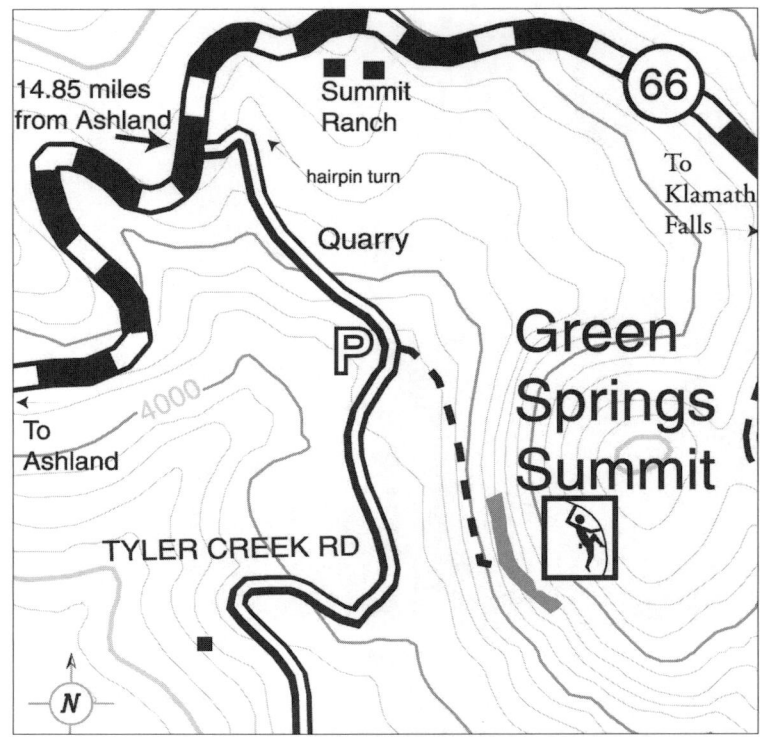

T40S, R03E, Section 5, WGS83 10T⁵ 42 ²³²ᵐ E.⁴⁶64¹³⁵ᵐ N.

How To Get There

From Interstate 5 take the second Ashland exit (Exit 14). Head east past the Ashland Hills Inn onto Greensprings Highway (Highway 66). Follow Greensprings Highway south past Emigrant Lake, 14.8 miles to Tyler Creek Road. Tyler Creek Road will be on the right. Follow Tyler Creek Road for about a quarter mile down the steep hill, around the hairpin curve, and past the quarry on your left, until you come to the first large pullout (large enough for 4 to 5 cars) on the right side of the road. Continuing beyond this pullout takes you around an "S" turn and the driveway of 420 Tyler Creek Road off to the right. Locate the Greensprings access trail directly across the road from the pullout. This short trail contours the hill at a 50% grade. Steps that were constructed in the 1990's are in need of maintenance. Follow the trail through the reproduction unit and up the hill for a brisk five-minute walk to emerge at the middle section of the Greensprings columns. The trail forks off with the Marge Column (reference A) about 200 feet to the left and the right section (reference D) to the right.

Average length = 45 feet

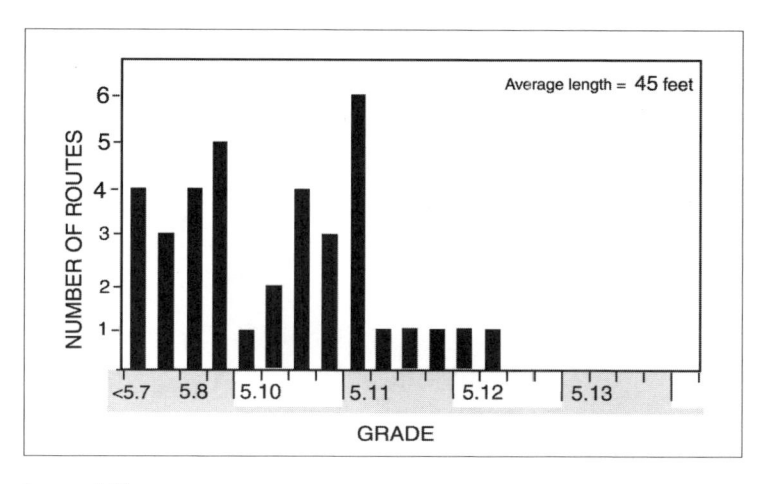

Left Wall

(Topo A1, A2 and B)

To approach Left Wall follow the main trail to its junction at the base of the cliff (Middle Wall). From here walk approximately 75 feet left up a short steep slope to the large flat belay boulder below the Left Wall. Marge's Hairdo can be seen to the far left.

1a Marge's Naval **5.8

Marge's Navel climbs up the face of Marge spire staying out of the large crack to the right and ends at the first set of belay anchors. This oddly bolted and puzzling face often baffles 5.8 climbers. Marge's "Navel" above the fifth bolt is a truly cool feature. FA unknown.

1b Full Marge **5.11a

Climb Marge's Navel and ponder the strength of Marge's neck as you pull onto the teetering pillar above. 80 feet with bolts.
FA Joe Chaves, bolted by Bill Newcomb.

2 Marge Simpson's Backside **5.6

Follow dual cracks up into the chimney onto the right side face to its summit. One bolt protects the route across the face to the summit.
FA Gavin Ferguson.

3 Six Cheetas ****5.10c

This route features the longest section of continuously overhanging rock at the Greensprings. The final moves traverse right at the ledge to climb the arete and face just left of "Boys". Take care not to knock down rubble from the ledge. Nine bolts. FA Joe Chaves, Spring 2001.

4
Boys Who Ain't French
****5.11b

First bolted line at Greensprings. An excellent route which remains a testament to the thoughtfulness of its first ascent party. Climb direct to first bolt. These moves will be straight forward with solid holds. The crux is located slightly above the forth bolt. Stay off arete to left and Sky Patrol to the right.
FA Jim Smallwood.

5
Sky Patrol
****10a(R)

A classic Greensprings crack climb on lead or toprope. This route is mostly 5.8 with a 5.10a crux at the top. The crux requires small gear to 1 inch and is difficult to protect.

6
Procrastinating Aliens
5.7

Procrastinating Aliens follows a dirty double crack system up the gully right of Sky Patrol.

7
Alien Life Forms
5.7

Climb Procrastinating Aliens using only the right-hand crack.
FA Don Ransom, 1982.

8
Loose Ends
****5.11c

Approximately 80 feet in height, Loose Ends is one of the longest lines at Greensprings.

9
Hairway to Steavan
****5.10c/d

This route climbs the left side of the outer column immediately above the flat belay boulder. The first 20 feet may contain the best climbing at Greensprings. This is a route that yields to genius before strength. FA Cory Jones.

Greensprings 89

Preceding page,
Jessica Drake
(10) on Marge's
Backside (5.6).
Don Asay

Topo A1
Side view of the
Marge Collumn.

Rogue

Greensprings

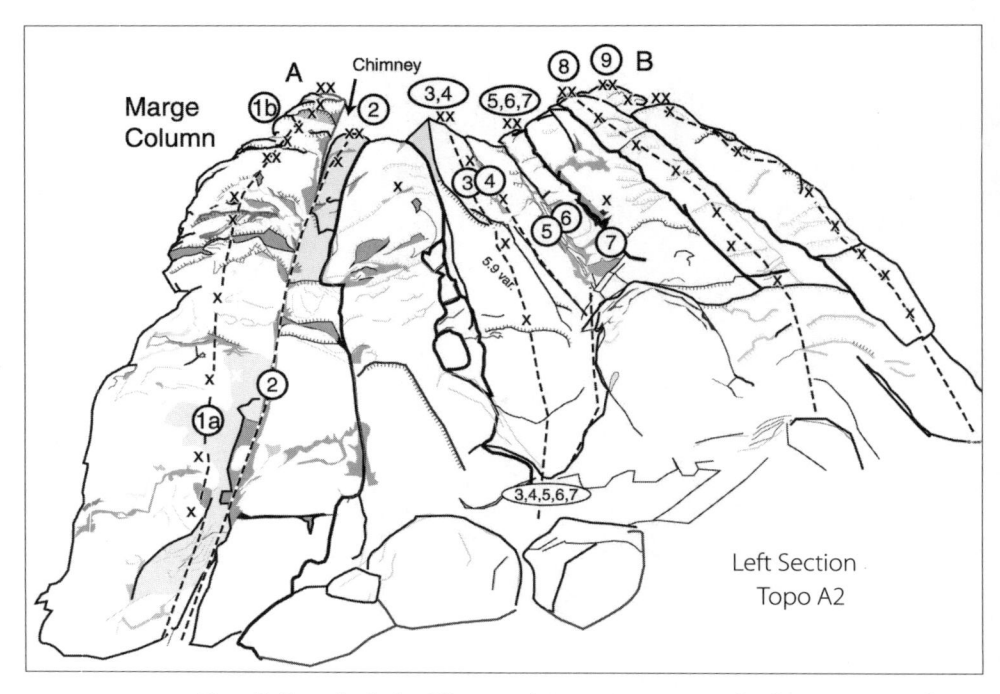

Left Section
Topo A2

10
Chain Links
5.10c w/ 5.8 var

Follow the bolted line up this consistent 5.10 climbing. Crux is above the fourth bolt. Using the crack to the right creates a 5.8 variation.

11
Deep Purple
5.9

Climb to the summit staying in the crack feature to the right side of the Chain Links arete.

12
Greenscreams
****5.11c

This is an exciting route with multiple crux moves involving delicate smearing, aggressive high steps, and technical moves on small holds. Crux begins above first bolt.
FA Dan Higgins and Cory Jones.

13
Ski Tracks
5.10a/b

Flared crack that is somewhat difficult to protect. Toprope recommended.

Greensprings 91

Right Side of Left Section
Topo B

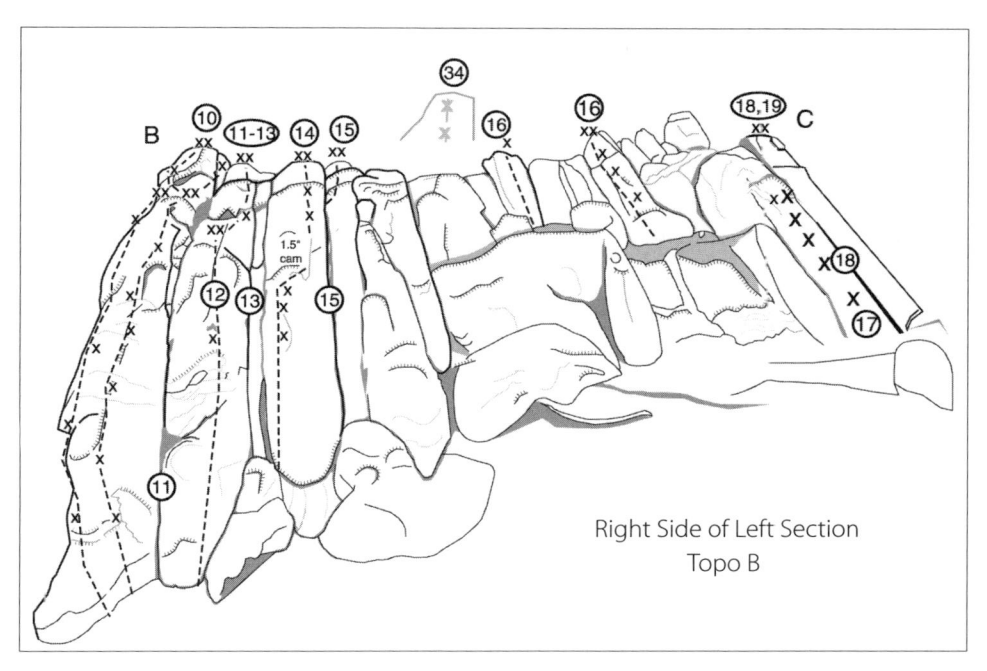

14	Fun but frightening with an R rating for those who don't stick clip the first bolt. Climb starts on the face to the right of Ski Tracks. The crux involves hidden side-pulls and tenuous smears in route to the first clip. A large Pocket half way up and the horizontal crack near the top can be protected with gear less than 2.5 inches. This route is not set up for convenient lowering as the anchor bolts are set back somewhat from the top of the route and are not equipped with chain. Bring long slings for the anchor if you wish to toprope.
Knobland	
**5.10c	

15	Also known as Loose Flake, this route follows a widening crack system, leading right onto the face. Although not recommended, this route is often top-roped using a Mahogany bush at the top as an anchor. Beware of detached pillar. Gear to 2.5 inches.
Snake-N-Flake	
5.7	

16a	Abandoned project, top anchor hanger removed.

16b	A short three bolt route. Start from the large ledge. FA Cory Jones.
Jonser	
5.10b/c	

Rogue

Greensprings

Topo C
Middle Section

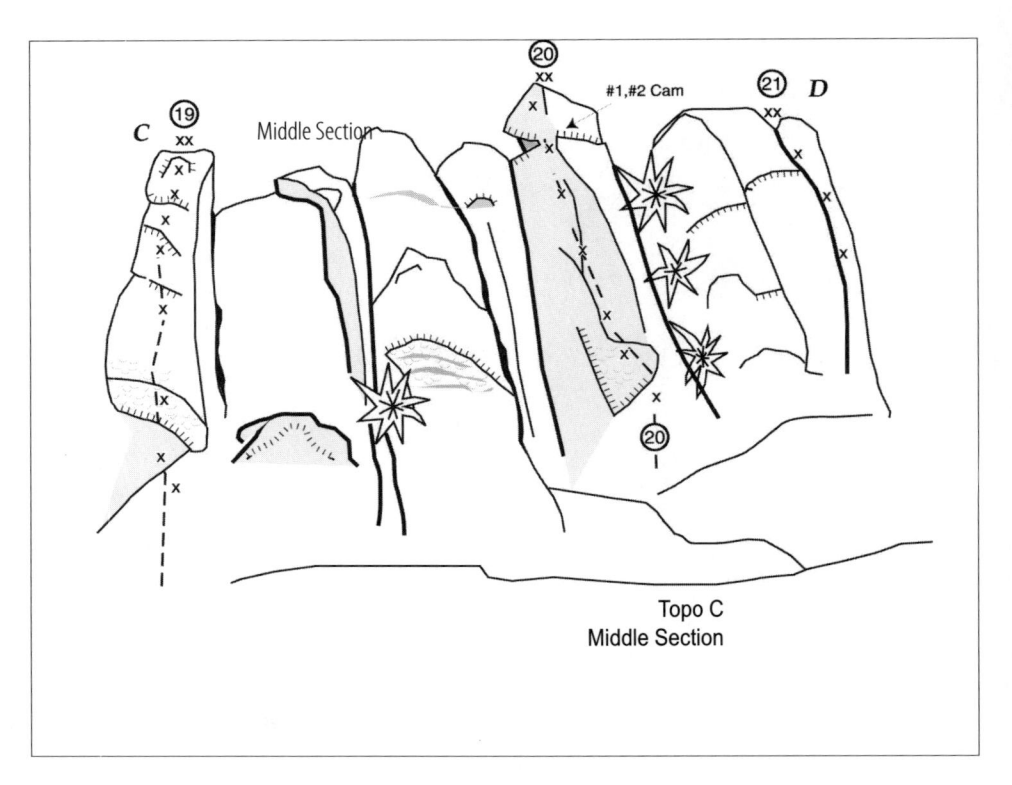

17 Shadowlands ***5.11c — Starts on the large ledge behind the old growth Douglas-fir. The first move will yield only to those with the patience of Job. Difficulties ease slowly as one ascends. 40 feet with 4 bolts. FA Joe Chaves, 2000.

18 Off-width ***5.8 — An excellent climb up the off-width crack to the left of Keep the Fat. Establishing a toprope requires a 5th class down climb over dirty rock.

Middle Wall
(Topo C)
The Middle Section is the first face you will see when you reach the rock cliff from the access trail.

19 Keep the Fat ***10d — Recently rebolted this route climbs the face of the farthest left column on the middle section of Greensprings and will be directly to your left as you approach the columns from the access trail.
FA Joe Chaves.

Greensprings

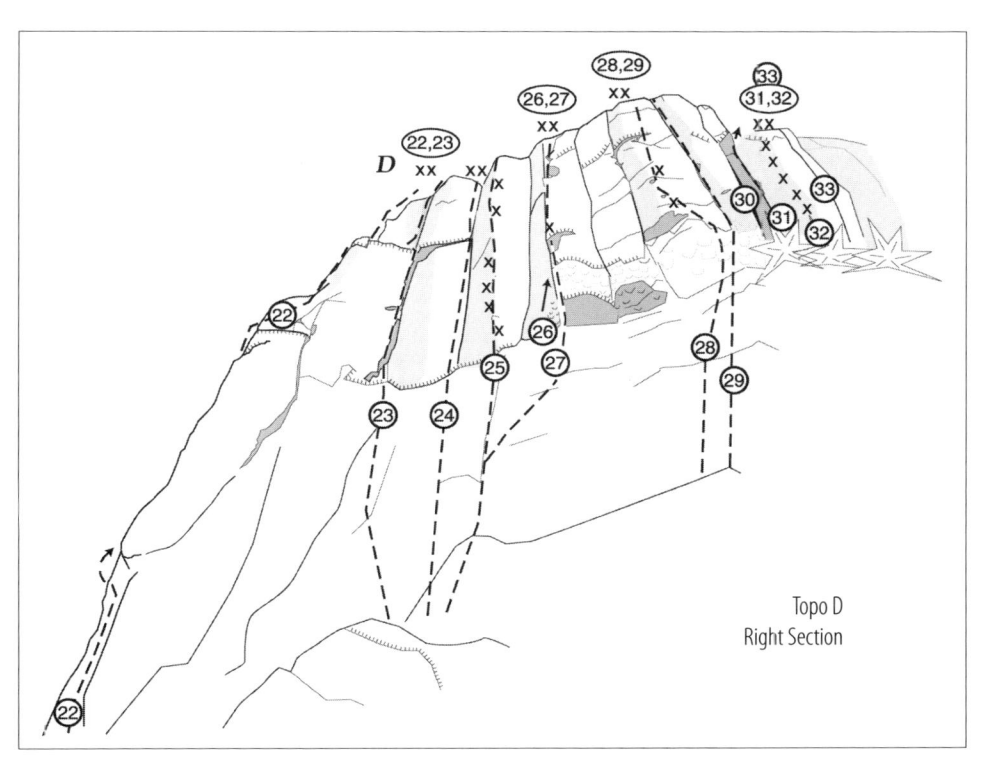

Topo D
Right Section

20
Mexican Summer
***5.11a

This is the only route at Greensprings requiring a 60-meter rope. The start is simple but dirty. Mexican Summer features consistently cool moves and would be one of the top five routes here if rebolted. FA unknown.

Right Section
(Topo D)

21
Mountain Jam
**5.9

Two pitches, this route is protected with bolts at the beginning, finishing the first pitch with a dihedral/crack system. The second pitch ascends an obvious crack to your left twenty feet to the top.

22
Blitzfart
**5.9

Two pitches, it begins just left of Razor Crack and climbs a thin crack to the ledge. From the ledge continue up the crack to the top. No bolts.

Rogue

**23
Razor Crack
****5.8, 5.11 var.**

A Greensprings classic. Good holds always appear when you need them most. Really excellent 5.11 variation is to stem without using the crack. One of only a few opportunities for such climbing in southern Oregon. FA unknown.

**24
Last Chance
****5.12b**

This highly technical route ascends a barren arete just to the right of Razor Crack. It requires aggressive smearing and ingenious laybacks. FA Dan Higgins.

**25
Test Tube
5.10c

This route climbs the dihedral right of Last Chance. Climb directly up the dihedral placing pro in Yosemite Crack to the right. This route is smooth and clean below, easier and often vegetated above. The holdless crux will test your stemming abilities. Two bolt anchor with chains, on top. Protect with gear.

**26
Yosemite Crack
5.11+

This tidy looking crack right of Test Tube comes with a guarantee of intense pain to all who would attempt it. A proper ascent contrives to climb the crack directly without stemming.

**26.5
Free Goo
5.11b

Free Goo climbs the bulging arete immediately right of Yosemite Crack. You may not be thrilled with the moves, but as Homer would say, "mmm, free goo". 4 bolts. FA Joe Chaves, Summer 2001.

**27
Kooch Master
***5.11a**

Have fun testing your ape index at the wild crux passing the first bolt. The upper moves are thin and sustained. FA Gavin Ferguson.

**28
Paul's Crack
5.9**

Climb the crack just right of Kooch Master. No top anchors, gear to 3 inches.

**29
Chimney
5.6**

Protect using gear to 12 inches deep in crack. Can be toproped.

**30
Thin Crack
5.10d

Follow the very thin and dirty flare crack just left of Euphoria. Toprope.

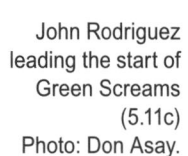

John Rodriguez
leading the start of
Green Screams
(5.11c)
Photo: Don Asay.

"The artist must atune himself to that which wants to reveal itself a permit the process to happen through him."
—*Martin Heidegger*

Rogue

Nick Asay on Sky Patrol (5.10a). Photo: Don Asay

31
Euphoria
***5.11a

One of the first bolted climbs at Greensprings, the history of Euphoria is one of chopped bolts and controversy. Closely placed anchors and really thin moves make Euphoria a fun route. Stay out of the right hand crack for a 5.11 lead. FA Jim Smallwood, Dan Higgins.

32
Axe Wound
***5.6

Just right of Euphoria, this pleasant crack has a difficult beginning, finishing with large holds. Protect with gear to 3.5 inches.

33
Inflatable Man
**5.10d

This short two bolt lead ascends a short face on the second level immediately above Euphoria. No anchors.
FA Jim Smallwood

Route Descriptions courtesy Joe Chaves and (Nicholas A. Dodge, 1968).

Pilot Rock is a shallow intrusive rhyolitic volcano plug that sits on top of the Siskiyou. Its formations of columns tilt 20 to 30 degrees to the Northeast from the uplift forces that shape the Siskiyou. Loose columns and loose rock on top have limited most of the route development to only a small area on the south side and two earlier routes on the southwest side. A well-worn trail leads from the Pacific Crest Trail to Pilot's West Gully Route. With Mount Shasta rising to the south and Mount McLoughlin to the north, both the columnar formations and view from the top of Pilot Rock are spectacular. Note: Climbing columns has inhernt risks. Columns should be evaluated each season for stability as columns that are stable one season, may not be stable the following season.

In 1968, Nicholas Dodge recorded 7 climbs and scramble routes on Pilot Rock. The most popular of these routes remains the Class-3 *West Gully* up the west gully that takes hikers to spectacular spiritual views on top the summit. Only two of the original routes are described here. Five additional routes established after1988, dominated by the efforts of Chuck Porter and Joe Chaves provide exceptional climbing up spectacular columns.

Rogue

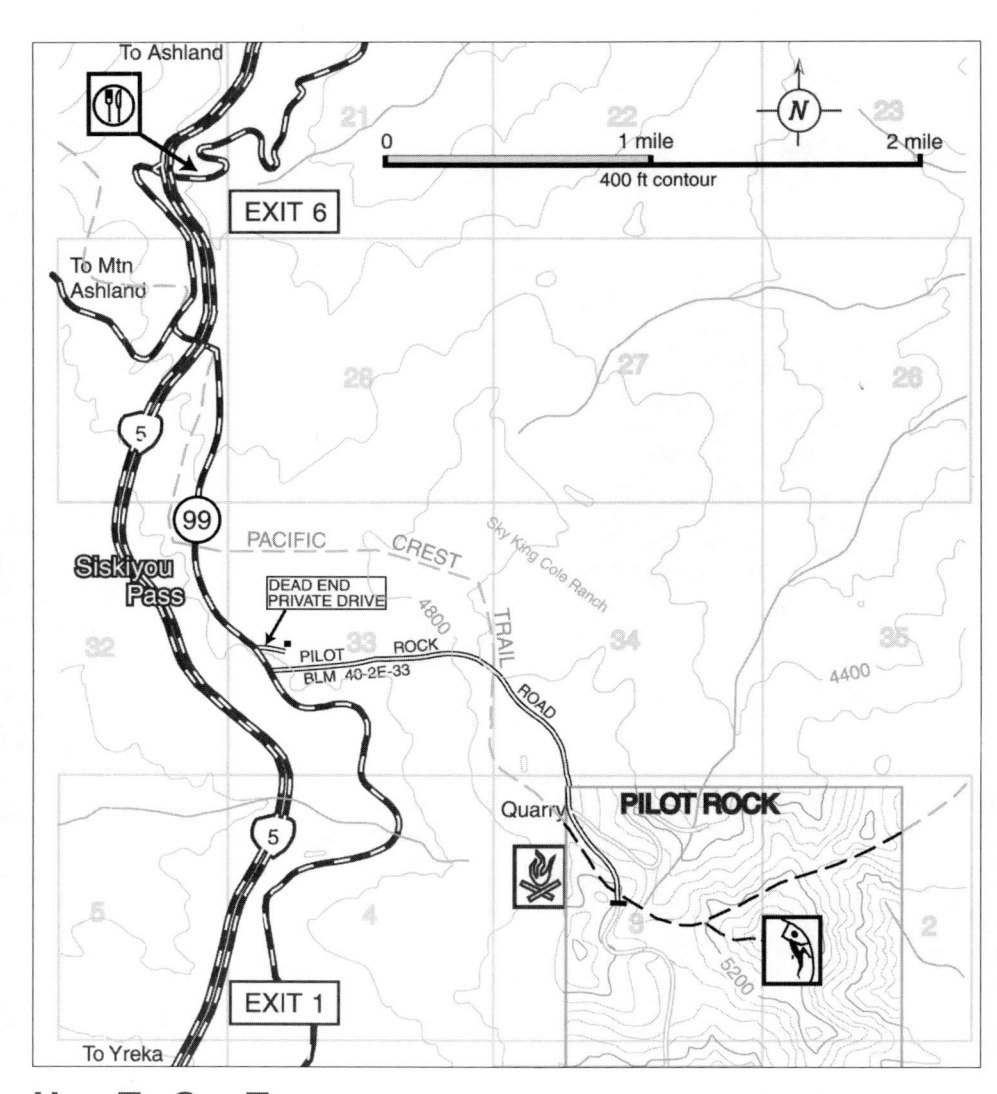

How To Get There

Travel 8 miles from Ashland, south on Interstate 5 to Siskiyou Pass. Take Exit 6, continuing south on Old Siskiyou Highway 99 past the Mount Ashland turnoff and under Interstate 5. Continue on Highway 99 for about 3 miles to the top of the Siskiyou. Turn left onto Pilot Rock Road (BLM 40-2E-33), as Highway 99 starts down the south slope. Follow Pilot Rock Road as it climbs and follows the north crest of the Siskiyou and ends at an earthen roadblock and the Pacific Crest Trail. Hike several hundred feet east along the Pacific Crest Trail turning right onto a well-worn 10 foot wide trail that continues on along the ridge top to Pilot Rock.

Pilot Rock

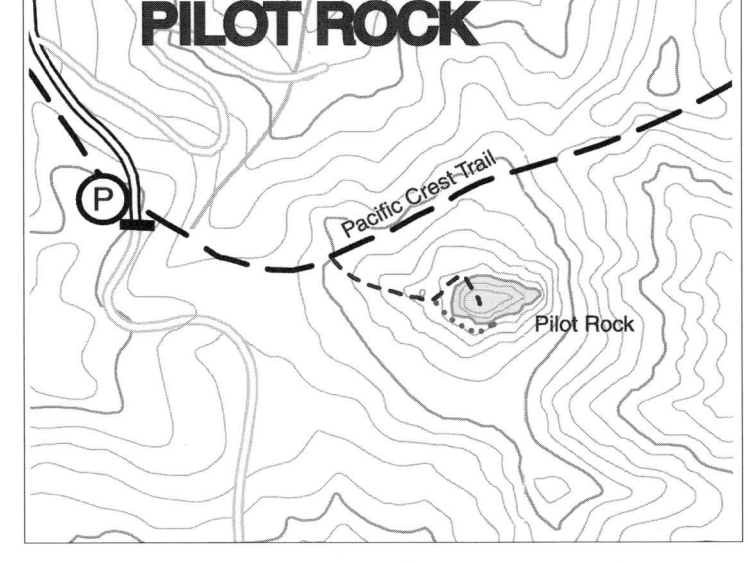

WGS 84 10 T $^{5}36^{369m.}$
E. $^{46}53^{266m.}$ N.

Willamette Meridian,
T41S, R02E,
W 1/2 of Section 2.

There are currently at least twelve established routes on Pilot Rock. A number of these are not of interest to most climbers due to poor quality and are not described here. The average length of these routes is 275 feet. They range in difficulty from Class 3 to 5.11a. All routes require gear placements. Pilot Rock has a lot of loose rock so wearing a helmet is highly recommended and experience is essential.

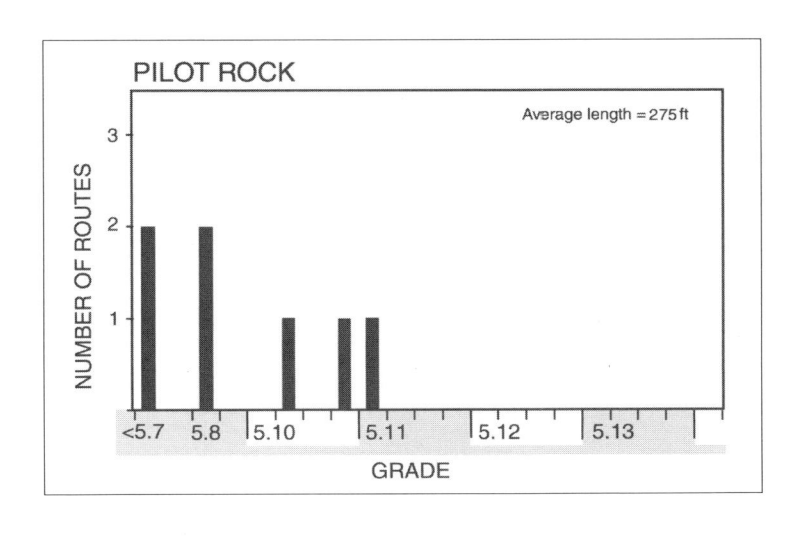

The Rogue

Pilot Rock

Caution:
Loose Blocks
xx fp
fp

1
West Gully
Class 3

From the parking area, hike northeast about two to three hundred feet up the Pacific Crest Trail (PCT). As the PCT starts to contour down the north side of Pilot Ridge there will be a 10 foot wide well defined scramble trail on the right that follows the crest of the ridge up to Pilot Rock. Follow this trail to the large rock shoot/gully that opens up on the west face of Pilot Rock. Scramble up the gully to the summit. There are two 6 to 8 foot drops that offer a challenge, especially when down climbing. This is a beautiful route through Pilot Rocks columnar formation. FA unknown

2
Southwest Arete
5.8

Scramble the sloping ramp from the *West Gully* to the base of the south arete. The South Arete has one fixed piton at its base and two as a top belay. Evaluate the quality of these anchors before relying on them, but don't remove as they mark the route. About three fourths of the way up locate a sling rapped around a column. FA unknown, pre 1980's.

3
Roundabout
**** 5.10d

The first pitch of this route may be the most enjoyable on Pilot Rock. It is clean, well protected, and airy. All belay stances are bolted.

Pitch-1: (5.10a) Climb straight up over four bulges placing gear and clipping 5 bolts. Climb "roundabout" at the third bolt. Traverse right 15 feet after fifth bolt. Sling a horn between the final fifth bolt and the belay. 100 feet with 5 bolts, a 0.75 Camalot, small gear, and a sling for the horn just before the belay anchors. A 60-meter rope will reach the ground.

Pitch-2: (5.10d) Ascend up and left through the crux bulge and a large white scar above. Climbing becomes 5.7 or so above the crux. Small cams essential at the crux (i.e. blue and yellow TCU). 150 feet with 5 bolts.

Pitch-3: (5.7) Climb left and up to a 3-bolt belay. Use gear and 3 bolts on route to protect. 65 feet. FA Joe Chaves and Pat Uhtoff.

4
Crash Landing
*** 5.8

Two pitches using gear and bolts. Watch out for loose rock. Pitch-1: First pitch climbs up two separate columns. The belay bolts ontop the first pitch are placed on an entirely detached column and should be moved. 100 feet (5.8), gear to 1-1/2 inches with 6 bolts. Pitch-2: Traverse left into a chimney (5.6) and end at second anchor. 160 feet, gear to 3 inches with 4 bolts. All belays are bolted. Crash Landing is the preferred south side descent route. FA Chuck Porter

Joe Chaves on pitch-2 of Magic Blocks. Greg Orton

Above and facing page: Southwest Face of Pilot Rock.

5
Magic Blocks
**** 5.11a

Three pitches using gear and fixed anchors. Route begins on a large belay pad immediately below a huge roof. 250 feet.
Pitch-1: (5.10b) 100 feet with 4 bolts, gear placements to 2 inches.
Pitch-2: Pull the roof (5.11a) on jugs, bolt at waist level. Climb becomes 5.7 above roof. 60 feet gear to 1 inch, 2 bolts.
Pitch-3: (5.10a) Start by traversing left 10 feet to an orange prow. Then climb up and right through clean bulges and a final somewhat loose one. 100 feet, gear to 1 inch with 3 bolts. FA Joe Chaves and Chuck Porter, 1998.

Pilot Rock 103

6
Step Up
*** 5.10b

Three pitches using gear and fixed anchors. Pitch 1: Start atop an 8-foot tall detached, leaning column (5.9ow). Ascend continuous off-width cracks separated at mid-height by a short traverse left. Belay from bolts behind an obvious 3-foot tall block. Gear to 4 inches, 100 feet. Pitch 2: (The Funhouse Pitch, 5.10b) This well-protected pitch leans weirdly through the first 5 bolts then traverses left over easier but somewhat crumbly rock to the Magic Blocks belay ledge. 70 feet protected with 8 bolts, no gear necessary. Pitch 3: (5.7) Traverse right 10 feet and ascend to summit. 90 feet gear to 1 inch, 4 bolts. Watch out for loose rock. FA Chuck Porter

7 - Pilots License
5.6

Two pitches up a pronounced gully to the right of Step Up using gear. No fixed anchors.
FA unknown.

The Rogue

Joe Chaves on pitch 2 of Magic Bocks (5.11a). Greg Orton

J. Messinger, D. Ransom, J. Chaves

Rabbit Ears sits prestigiously at the head of the Rogue River watershed basin, 5,600 feet above sea level. Rabbit Ears, is a shallow-intrusive volcanic plug of andesitic or dacitic composition. Magma cooled below the surface and the surrounding volcano eroded away leaving behind the 400-foot high East and West Ears and the large Lower Apron that distinctly resembles a rabbit's head.

Rabbit ears currently has 20 routes with an average route height of 150 feet. It has a good assortment of multi-pitch and single-pitch routes ranging from 5.5 to 5.11a. Nicholas Dodge (1968) recorded 1921 to be the first known ascent of the East and West Ears by White and Layton. Loose and poor rock quality on top the ears have prevented most routes from summitting. Rock quality on the Lower Apron is excellent providing opportunities for new 150-foot routes in the future.

In an effort to create nesting habitat for introducing Peregrine Falcon to Rabbit Ears, the Forest Service has blasted a ledge, leaving a huge scar on the East Ear. Rabbit Ears currently has a seasonal nesting closure that extends between February 1 until 2 weeks after the young have fledged, or earlier if unoccupied. This closure will be extended until August in the absence of monitoring information or public interest.

106 Rabbit Ears

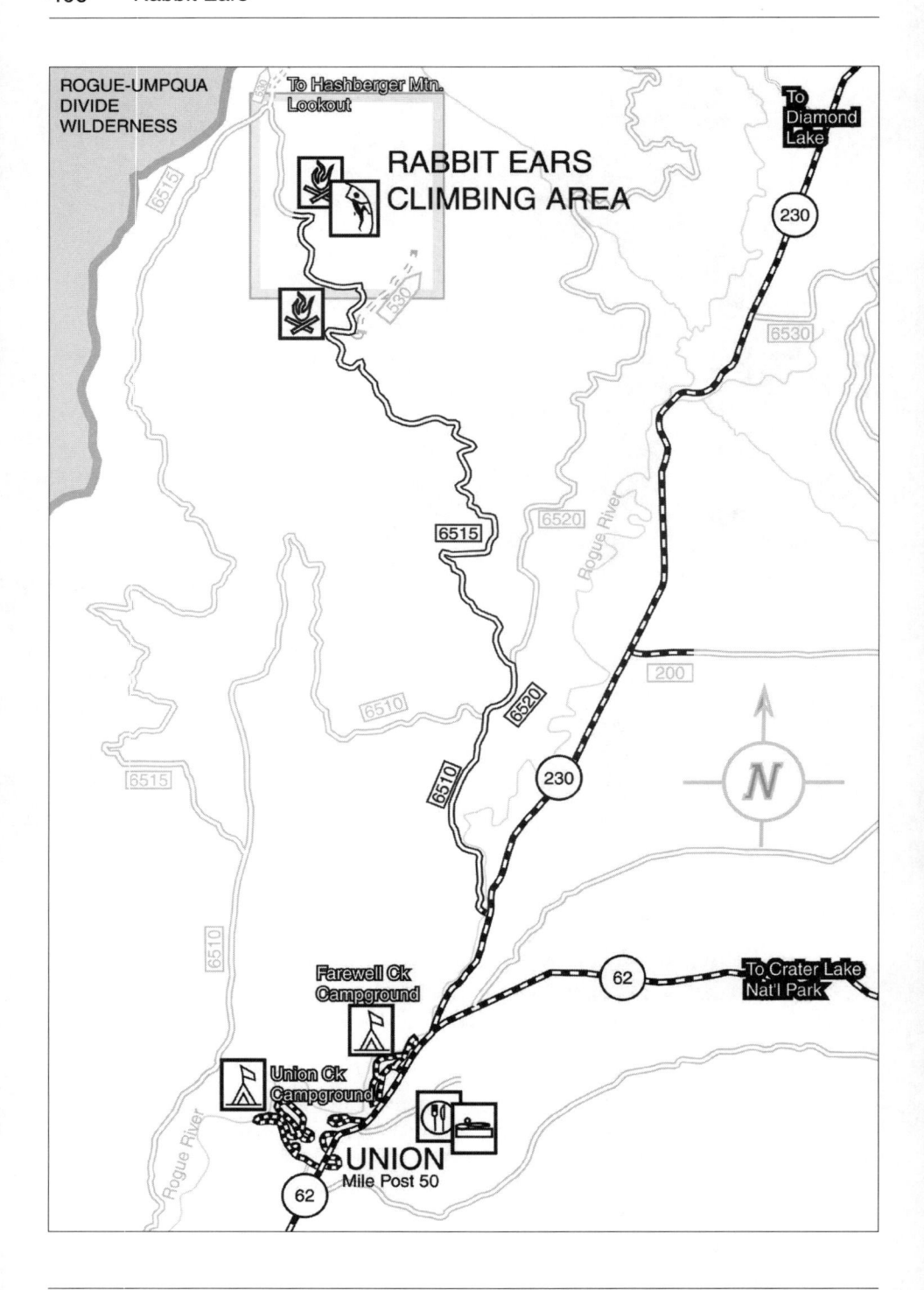

Rabbit Ears   107

How To Get There

✔ From Medford take Interstate 5 exit 30 onto Highway 62 north towards Union and Crater Lake National Park. After Union, continue north past the Crater Lake turnoff on Highway 230, taking the first left onto Forest Service Road 6510. (1.5 hours)

✔ From Roseburg drive east on Highway 138 to Diamond Lake. From Diamond Lake drive southwest on Highway 230 turning right onto Forest Service Road 6510 about half a mile before you come to Highway 66 and the Crater Lake turnoff. (2.75 hours)

✔ Take FS-6510 to FS-6520 and then left onto FS-6515 following the signs towards Hershberger Mountain Lookout. Continue up FS-6515 past the 530 spur-road. Rabbit Ears becomes visible from the road about 1.5 miles before you reach the tail head. As you approach the Rabbit Ears ridge you'll again loose sight of the rock. When you reach the ridge-top park in the large pullout on the right. An access trail follows the ridge for several hundred feet from the parking pullout to the West Ear. To access the Lower Apron traverse around the south side of the West Ear to the base of the east ear. Scramble south down a large bedrock gully to a trail that traverses east.

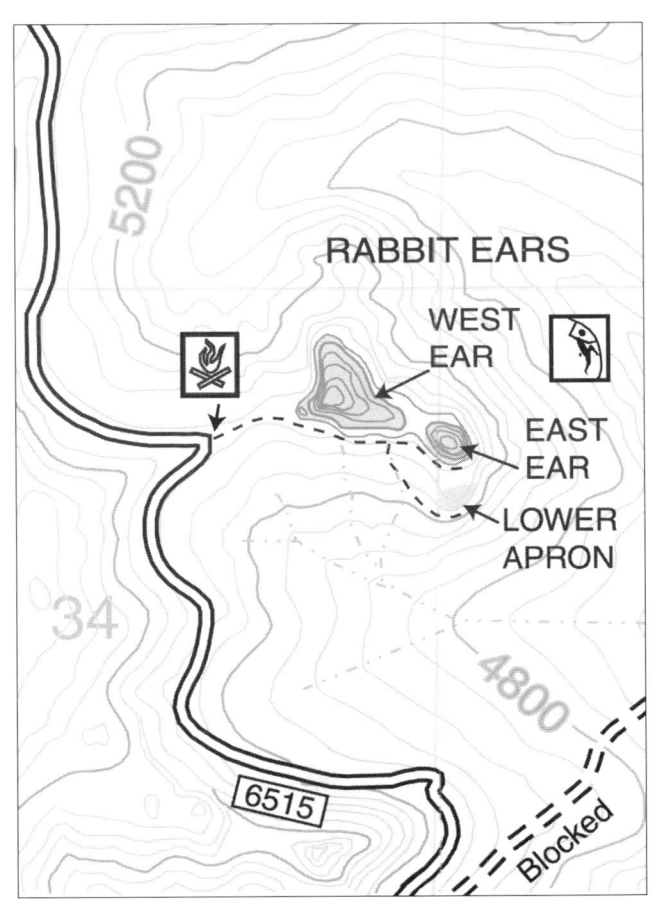

WGS 84 10T 545^{579m}·E., $476 1^{768m}$·N.

T29S, R03E, Sections 34 and 35, WM. Prospect Ranger District, Rogue River Nat'l Forest

Rogue

Rabbit Ears

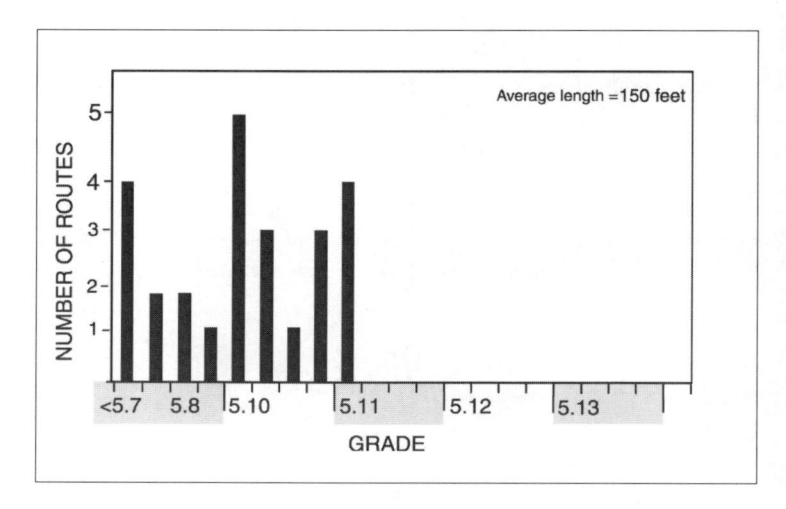

Average length = 150 feet

WEST EAR

1 West Chimney 5.6 (X) — From the access trail, the west chimney is the first feature you come to. The chimney itself is about 300 feet tall. *West Chimney* is a traditional route of marginal quality. Place your protection deep into the chimney as you climb. Climb the chimney into the saddle above (2 pitches). Set up a belay using the only tree in the saddle. From the tree climb the large crack to the summit. Towards the top the rock becomes loose and very marginal. From the summit, down climb or sling a horn and rappel down the east face. FA Unknown

2 West Ear Summit Routes **5.4-5.5 — Follow the trail from the base of the rock to the south side between the *West* and *East Ears*. Climb up the first obvious gully and at its head turn west to follow a gully system up the East Face. Climb directly up 100 feet, then onto one of the three of the obvious routes that climb up the south ridge, up the center, or up the north ridge. Climbing the north ridge is very exposed. To descend down climb or sling a horn and rappel down the east face.
FA W. White and M. Layton, 1921.

3 East Ear Summit **5.4-5.5 — The route up the East ear has great exposure. The rock is clean and not loose. Follow the trail around the West Ear beyond the first gully. The route goes up the west ridge. Descend the way you came up. FA W. White and M. Layton, 1921.

Rabbit Ears   109

Topo A: West Chiney Route

South Face of East Ear

Topo B. Follow the trail around the south side of the Rabbit Ears until you come to about the middle of the East Ear. Locate the snag near the base of the rock beneath a prominent ridge, 90 feet up. Polish Photo Route is the first route on the South Face. It climbs the buttress to the left side of a water mark.

4
Polish Photo Route
***5.7**
Approximately 40 feet west of a large snag. Begin at a bolt and climb the buttress as directly as possible. Climbing becomes easier as you pass into ground fall range. After you clip into the next bolt continue climbing to a 2-bolt belay making use of plentiful gear placements. FA Joe Chaves.

Rogue

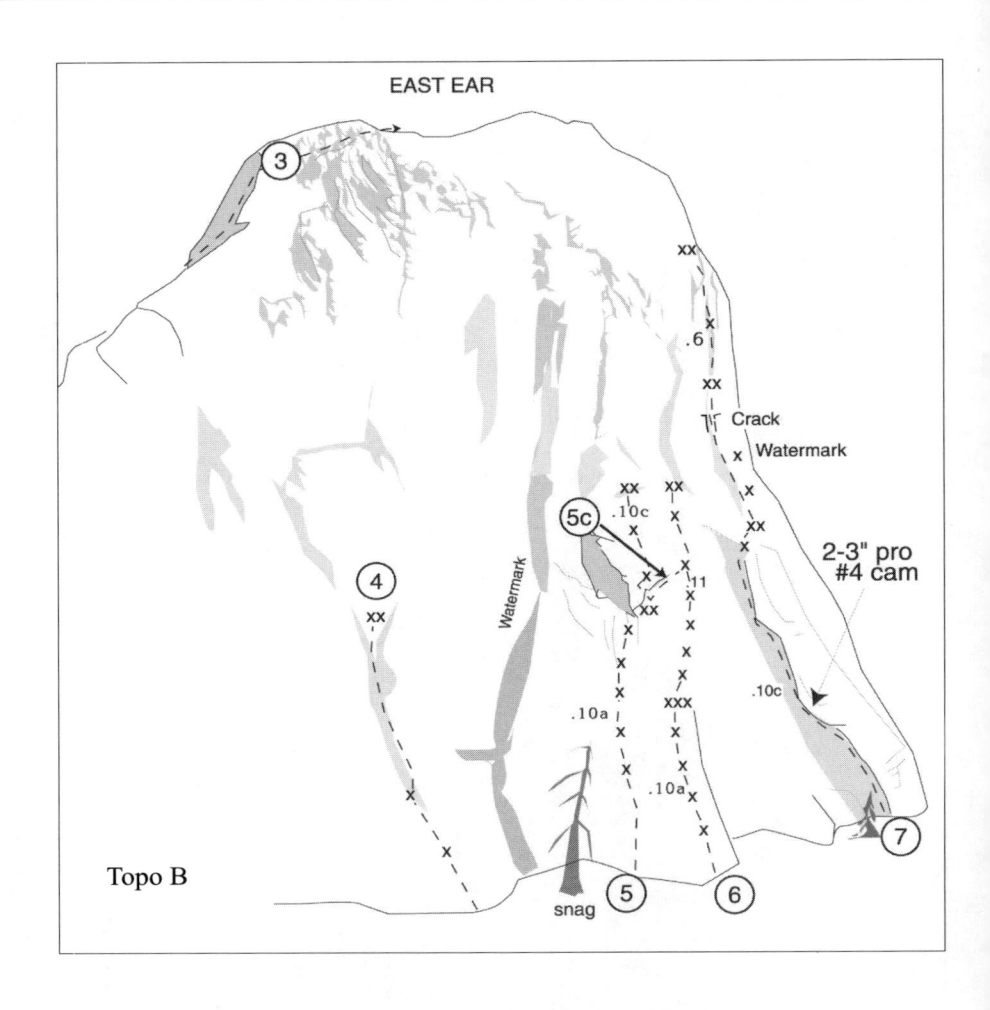

Rabbit Ears

5
Child's Play
****5.10c

Child's Play begins uphill from the base of the large snag.
Pitch 1: It's a long way to the first bolt, a stick clip will not reach. The rock here is sound with positive edges. Follow bolt line to a bolted belay at the base of a dihedral (5.10a). ~85 feet.
Pitch 2: (5.10c) climbs straight up and over the "*Hellbent Roof*" with 2 bolts and gear placement including a critical #2 Camalot lead to a bolt anchor. An excellent pitch! The rappel off is about 165 feet.

A variation (5c) is to make the *Hellbent Traverse* (5.10c), beneath the roof. Tie into *Gavin's Straight Up*, continuing up and left to the anchor for *Child's Play*. FA Joe Chaves

"Who has a fiercer struggle than he who strives to conquer himself."
— Thomas Kempis

Darryl Rasmussen on the lower appron. Josh Morell ©, imagethisphoto.com

6 Gavin's Straight Up ***5.10b-5.11a or A0

Pitch-1: The first pitch (10a) of this route was bolted by Gavin Ferguson over the course of several solo outings. As a result, the widely spaced bolt locations don't always correspond well with the current free variation. This is only a minor inconvenience to the climb, and Gavin's awesome efforts have opened up some excellent free climbing. 80 feet. FA Gavin Ferguson.

Pitch 2: Mostly bolts with some gear placements near the top. The two cruxes to this climb come a bit below the level of the *"Hellbent Roof"* and above as the route pitches back beyond vertical. Route traverses left just below the apron to finish at the Child's Play anchor. FA Joe Chaves.

7 Strange Force ****5.10d

Named for a deformed bit of gear once found on the first pitch.

Pitch 1: (5.10b) Follows the left facing dihedral with plentiful gear placements. At the point where the route turns to choss and the crack is less distinct, step right and clip a bolt. Continue right to a 2-bolt belay. 100 feet.

Pitch 2: (5.10c) Climb vertical to gently overhanging rock just right of a water streak passing 1 bolt on the way to a protectable water crack. Pull over onto a huge apron. Belay at 2-bolt belay. 70 feet.

Pitch 3: (5.6) Climb up and slightly left following a major line of weakness over clean rock. Pass 1 bolt on the way to a 2-bolt belay. ~120 feet. FA Joe Chaves and Chuck Porter, 1999.

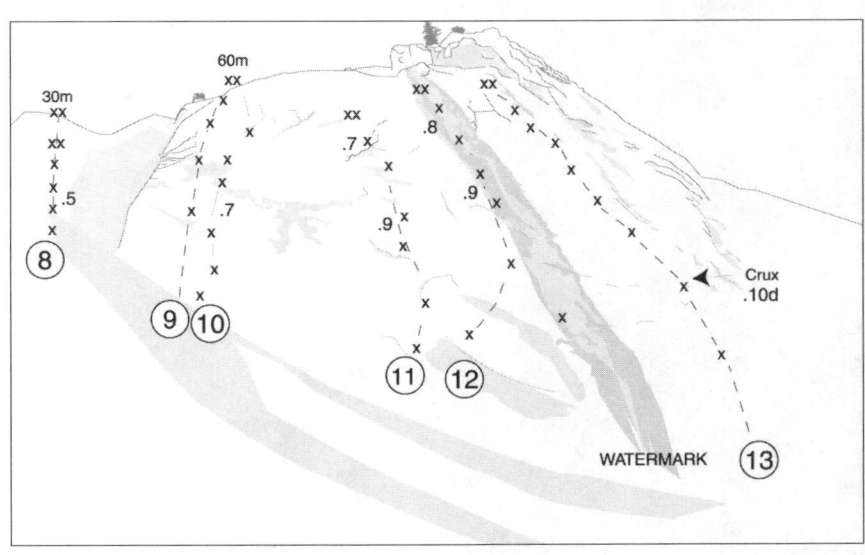

Topo C

Lower Apron
Topos C, D, and E
Follow the access trail from the parking pullout east along the ridge towards the West Ear. Follow the trail as it gradually descends beneath the south face of the West Ear eventually leading to a large area of easily traversable bedrock slabs. Traverse until directly beneath the notch between the ears, and then descend a broad, shallow gully util reaching a distinct trail that contours east to the west end of the slabs which form the lower apron. The rock quality here is excellent. The slaby dome has been polished by years of snow creep and the rock has a patina giving it unique quality. Watch out for old anchors and home made hangers on some of the older routes that still need to be upgraded. A good project for anyone interested in climbing here.

8
Lucky Rabbit's Foot
*5.5

Short 25-foot climb. Protected with 6 bolts.
FA Darryl Rasmussen and Bob Dowling, 2002.

9
Domes Do It
**5.7

Straightforward consistent 5.7 climbing on small edges and pockets. Old bolts that need replacing. Fun friction climb non-the less. FA (solo) Don Ransom, 1985.

10
Tricks are for Kids
***5.7

Climb right and direct with bolt line. Holds will appear when you need them. Shared top anchors with *Domes Do It*, 60m rope recommended.
FA Darryl Rasmussen and Bob Dowling, 2002.

11
Bowling for Bunnies
**5.8

Crux at third bolt where you'll find easier climbing a bit to the right (5.8/5.9).
FA Michael Lee, 1985.

12
Slippery When Wet
**5.9

Locate first bolt just right of Bowling for Bunnies. Climb up and right to second anchor at watermark. Crux is above second anchor on golden edges that can be a bit slick for 10 feet, then step right into watermark where you'll find better friction (when dry) and pockets to the top. FA Darryl Rasmussen and Bob Dowling, 2002.

114   Rabbit Ears

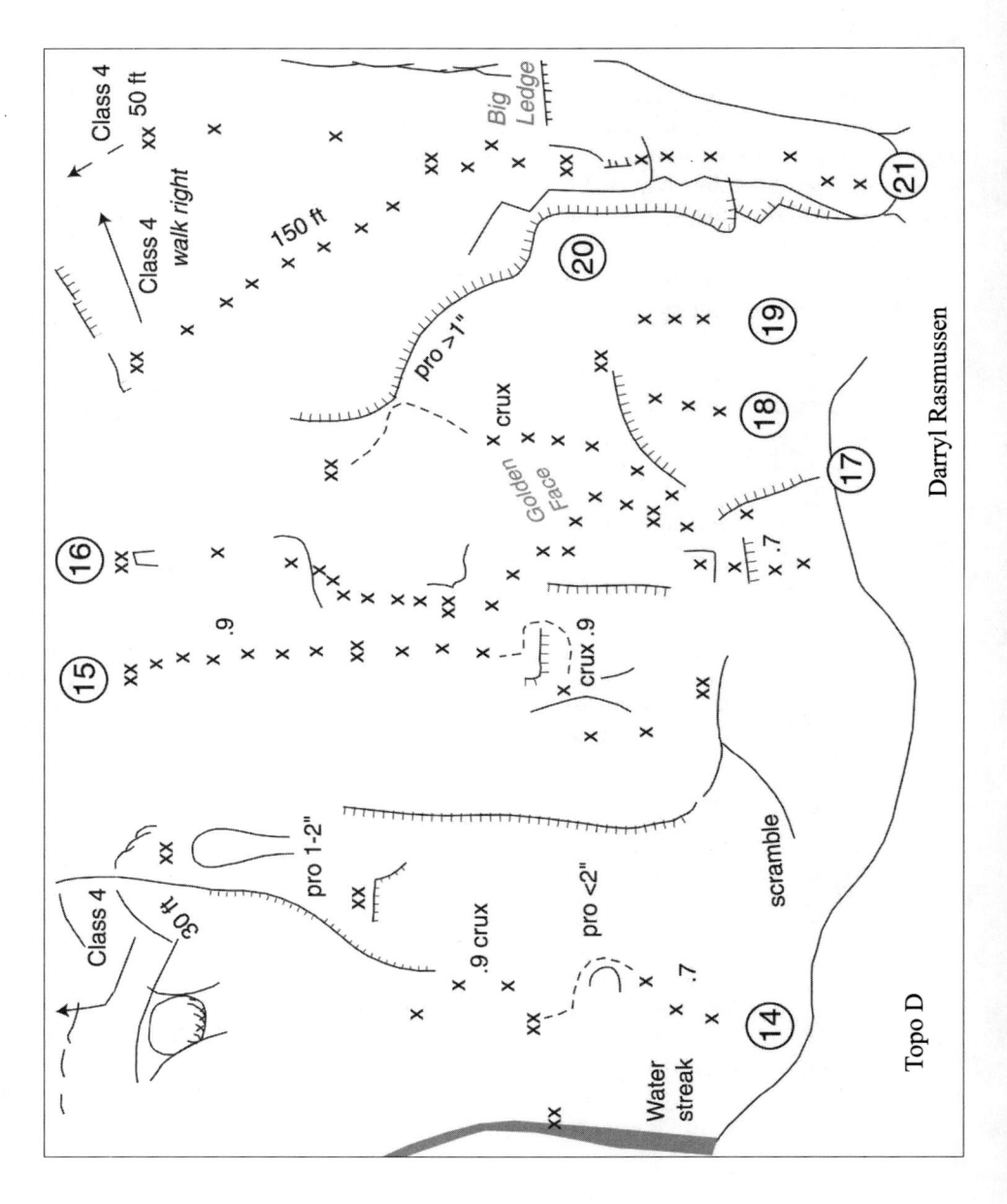

13 Sportholio ***5.10d — Climb to the right of the watermark. Crux is at second bolt. 110 feet with 9 bolts. Descend using a 60m rope. FA Joe Chaves and Sam Heismith, 1999.

14
Footloose
**5.10a

5.7 climbing to forth bolt. From forth climb left using the flake where you'll find placements up to 2 inch. Belay from anchors above flake. Pitch-2: Follow bolts to belay on ledge right of crack (5.9). FA Randy Benham and Don Ransom, 1985.

The Bowl
5.6-5.7
(Toprope)

Scramble, to the belay ledge from the uphill side. Climbs are approximately 25 feet high. The crux is just below the ledge where the rock steepens. Could be considered Class IV.

15
Tango n' Torture
**5.9

From the bowl climb through the steep water crack (crux), stepping right out of the water crack and the overhanging bulge to belay anchors just above. From this point follow the bolt line to the next set of double rappel anchors. Two sustained 5.9 pitches, each 95 feet. FA Mark Iverse and Steve Crews.

16
Crescent Gold
**5.10a

Pitch 1: climb up 60 feet into the right side of the bowl (5.7). FA Matt Weiseth. Pitch 2: Approx. 90 feet. Climb from right side of the bowl up and left around the overhang (5.9). Pitches 1 and 2 can be climbed together using a 6-meter rope. This avoids and uncomfortable belay ontop pitch 1. Pitch 3: Approx. 90 feet. Climb straight up following the bolt line. Crux (5.10a) is above third bolt at a well-protected steep wave. Rappel back down into the bowl. FA Matt Weiseth and Chris Sohl.

17
Slippery Gold
****5.10a (R)

The first unprotected 25 feet ranges from 5.6 to 5.7. A 5.8 bulge 30 feet up must be cleared before you reach the first bolt. After the first bolt the climbing becomes sustained 5.9 using thin edges and pockets with a 5.10a crux move after the fifth bolt. 160 feet. Rappel or climb off (5.9 X) with long runout to the top. FA Randy Benham and Don Ransom, 1985.

18
Pain
**5.11d

A short steep route just to the right of *Slippery Gold*. Shares top anchors with *Panic*. Approximately 25 feet protected with 3 bolts. FA Joe Chaves, 2001.

19
Panic
**5.10d

A short steep route just to the left of *Positively 4 Street*. Shares top anchors with *Pain*. Approximately 25 feet protected with 3 bolts. FA Joe Chaves, 2001.

20
Arching Crack
***5.10c

Climb the open-book using the crack for protection (5.9). Follow the *Arching Crack* past the chimney. Disregard an oddly placed bolt and traverse below the roof out to the top of *Slippery Gold's* first pitch (5.10c). The crux moves involves under-clinging the bombay off-width/chimney (5.10c). Gear is difficult to place, though solid placements are there. FA Unknown.

20b
Positively 4 Street TR
5.8 (R/X)

A variation of the *Arching Crack*, this route is very sustained and runout. Traverses left about 25 feet below the *Arching Crack*. Tops out at first pitch of Slippery Gold. FTR Don and Dylan Ransom.

20c

For a 5.8 (X) variation, follow the open-book to a chimney in the roof above. Leaving the crack following the chimney (5.8) will take you to the belay 5 feet above the chimney. Once you leave this crack the route is unprotected offering the potential for a 20 foot fall, with a bounce at 10 feet. FA Don and Dylan Ransom.

21
Arete
***5.10a

Follow bolt line up the arete. The crux is after the third bolt where you can bear hug a bulge and step right and around on a thin face. The last 15 feet requires placing protection in a thin crack or making a 5.8 runout. At third bolt a 5.8 variation is to move left into the Arching Crack. FA Dylan and Don Ransom, 1998.

22
Shag-Eared Villain
**5.11a (TR)

Project. Top rope the seam to the right of the arete. FTR Dylan and Don Ransom, 1998.

Rabbit Ears 117

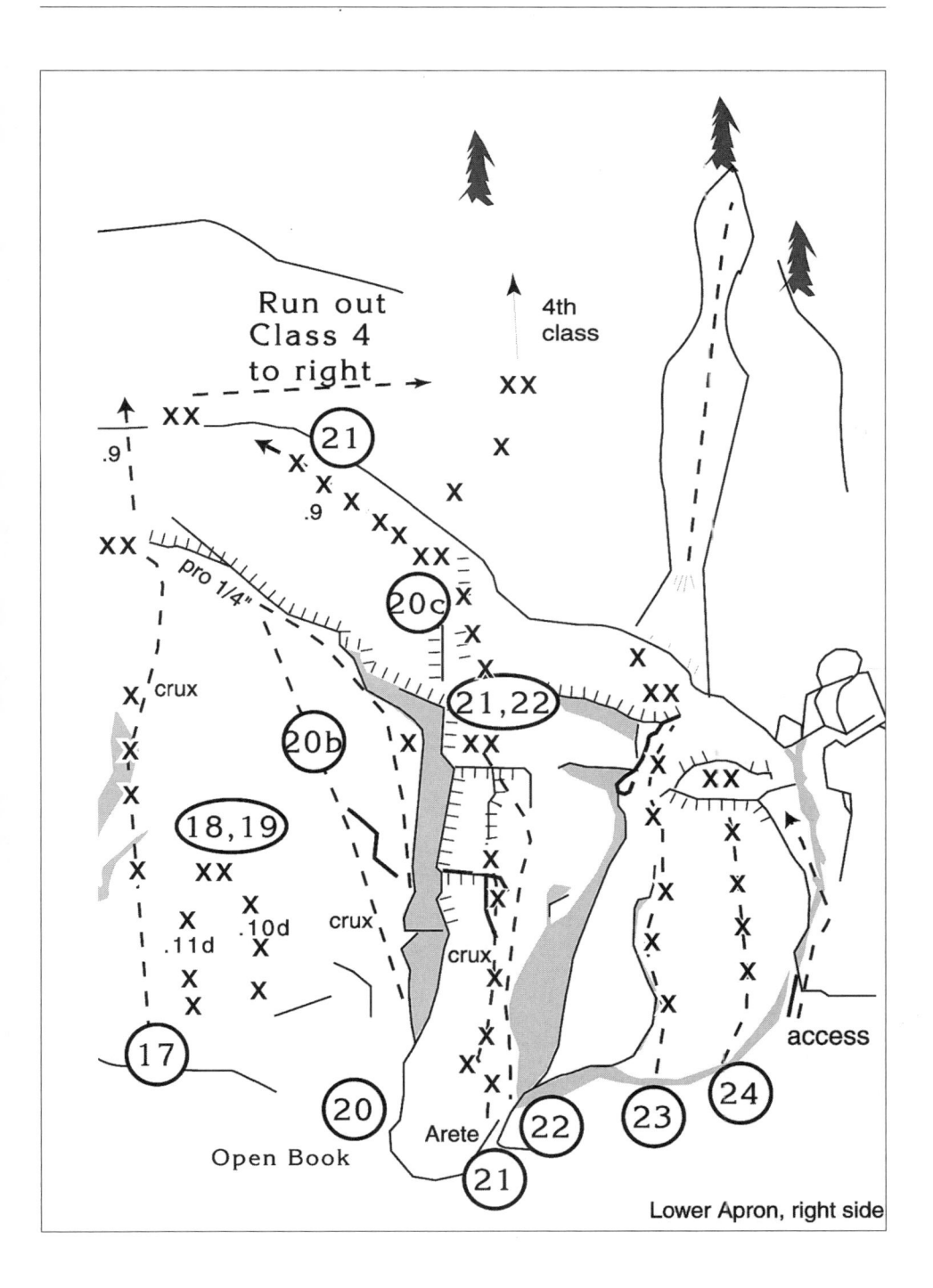

Run out
Class 4
to right →

4th
class

.9

pro 1/4"

crux

crux

crux

.11d   .10d

17

18,19

20b

20c

21,22

20
Open Book

21
Arete

22 23 24

access

Lower Apron, right side

Rogue

23
Velcro
(first pitch)
**5.10a (R)

Follow the bolt line along the left side of the face, to the left of the large ledge where *Rain Dance* tops out at, to the belay above. Once beyond the ledge the route makes a 25-foot runout with the potential to bounce. The lower half of *Velcro* can also top out at the large ledge to the right. This will allow you to finish before the runout. This section can also be easily toproped from the ledge.

Pitch 2 and 3: The second (5.7 X) and third (5.6 R) pitches (18b) offer a mediocre finish to an otherwise excellent route. There is only one bolt protecting the second pitch and none protecting the third. Dylan once took a 50-foot fall on the second pitch. FA Dylan and Don Ransom, 1998.

24
Rain Dance
****5.10a

Bolder the bottom 10 feet to first bolt. Cruxes are the bottom 10 feet and a bulge just past the third bolt. Both *Rain Dance* and the bottom portion of *Velcro* can be toproped from the ledge above. You can access this ledge by scrambling up the gully uphill from *Rain Dance*. FA Don and Dylan Ransom, 1999.

> "To climb up rocks is like the rest of your life, only simpler and safer."
> — *Charles E. Montague*

Rabbit Ears 119

Josh Morell ©, imagethisphoto.com

Rogue

Andy Eggleston on New Year's Day (5.10d), Rattlesnakes. Jerry Messinger.

Route descriptions by Jerry Messinger and Jim Davis

The rock of Rattlesnake is a welded tuff that varies in color from orange to purple. These 40 to 90 foot outcrops were formed from an avalanche of glowing hot ash, pumice, steam, and gasses that were expelled from a vent in the Board Mountain area. This material flowed from the flanks of a large volcano southwest of Rattlesnake, settling into a valley basin where it cooled. Now the rock at rattlesnake forms the rim rock along a narrow plateau, 3,200 feet above sea level.

Rattlesnake has a dry southeasterly aspect. The many Ponderosa pine and madrone in the area are part of the local ecology that is both adapted and prone to wildfire. When visiting the area follow all fire restrictions imposed by BLM or Boise-Cascade.

The Rogue

122 Rattlesnake

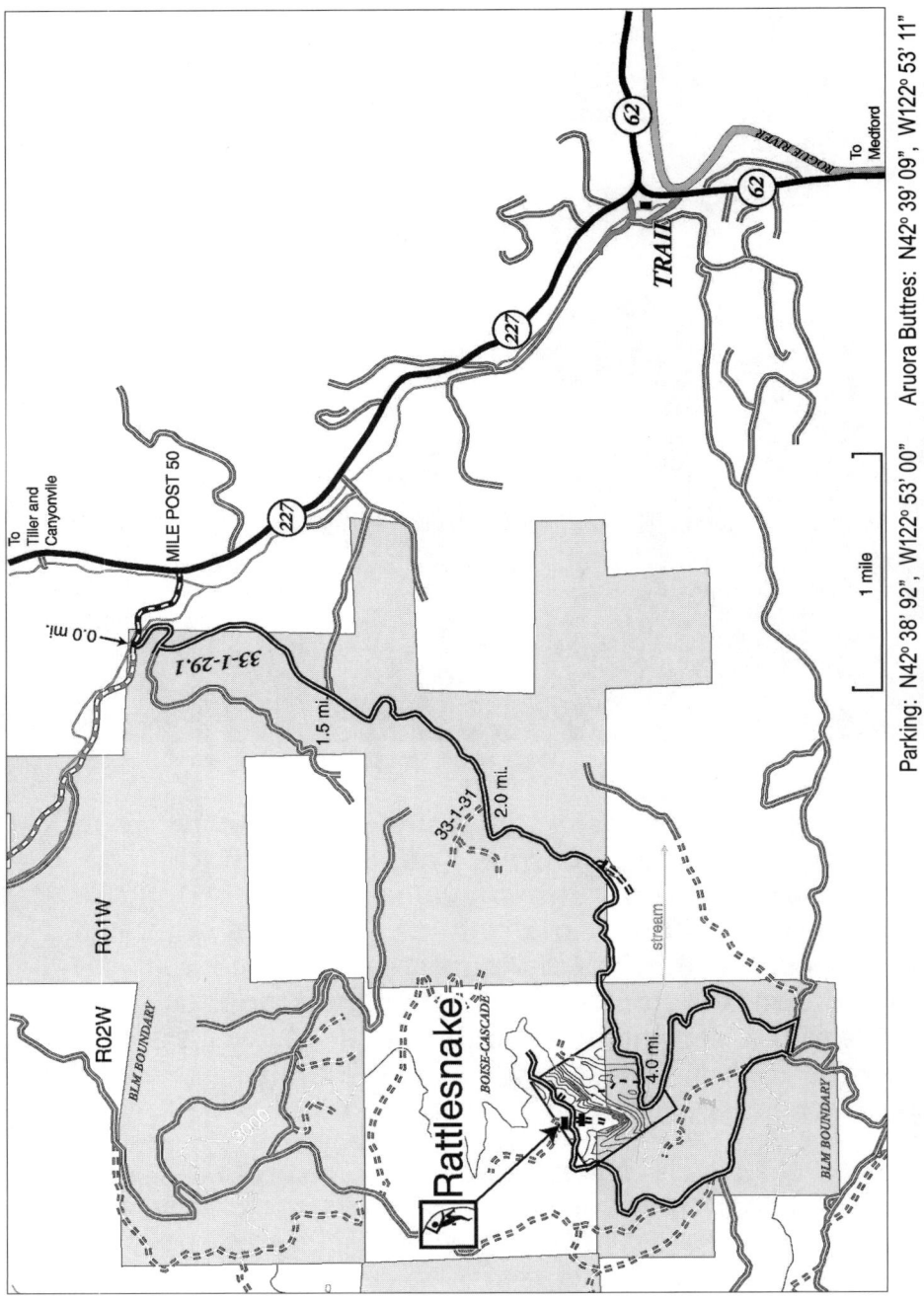

How To Get There

Rattlesnake is 45 minutes north of Medford and 1.75 hours from Roseburg. Shady Cove, on the edge of the Rogue River is 15 minutes from Rattlesnake and the closest full service community.

In Medford, from Interstate Highway 5, take Exit 30 and travel north towards Crater Lake on Highway 62 twenty-one miles to Trail.

✔ From Trail, turn left onto Highway 227. Head northwest on Highway 227 for three miles to Milepost 50. (Coming from the north on Highway 5, at Canyonville, take Highway 227 east for one hour to Milepost 50.)

✔ From Milepost 50, turn west onto the Trail Creek's West Fork Road. From the bridge, travel west for a 1/2 mile to where you will cross another smaller creek. Turn onto the first dirt road to your left and reset your odometer.

✔ Take this road for just a 1/4 mile and again take the first left turn you come to (BLM Road 33-1-29.1). BLM Road 33-1-29.1 bears right at 1.5 mile from the start of the dirt road.

✔ At 2.0 stay left again. At 3.0 you will round a sharp corner with a quarry to your right.

✔ Park in the pullout or if full, there are other pullouts nearby. An improved trail runs from the road west for several hundred yards up a draw to the base of Aurora Buttress. A lot of volunteer work has gone into constructing the trails around the Rattlesnake crag. They are in excellent condition and are easy to follow. BLM has asked climbers to self-regulate their activities at the crags. They have also asked that no new trails be constructed without prior approval.

Many of Rattlesnakes cliffs remain climbable throughout most of the winter.

124　Rattlesnake

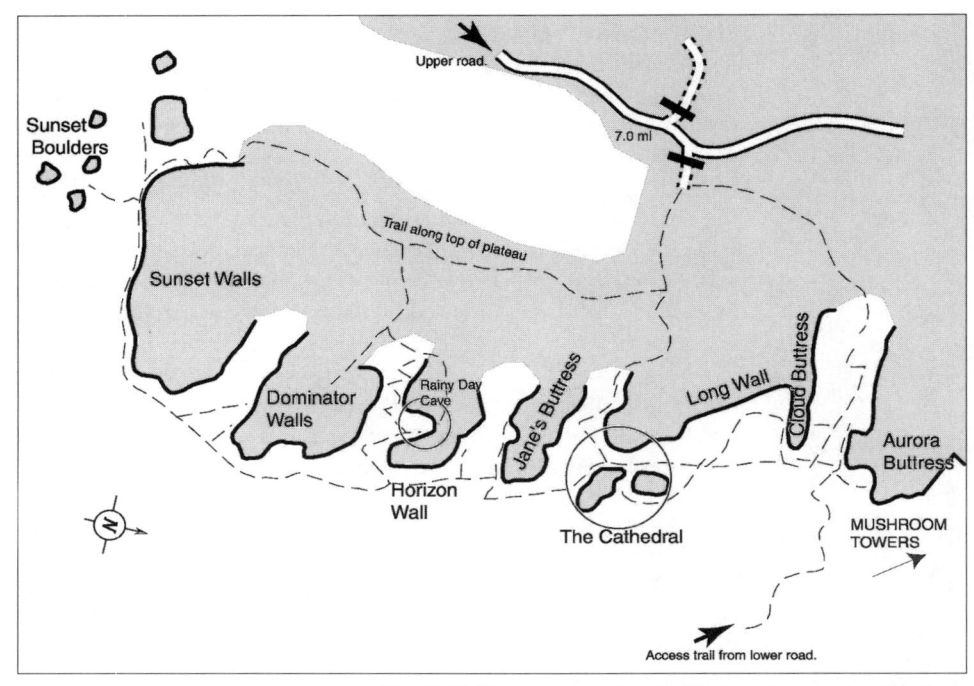

Map 2: Rattlesnake overview of cliff formations and trail system.

It is important when you are driving and parking along the 33-1-29.1 road that you remain alert for logging trucks. Park as far to the side of the road as you can, and do not take the center of the road when driving around turns. For tips about traveling mountain roads with truck traffic, please review the Safety section of the Introduction.

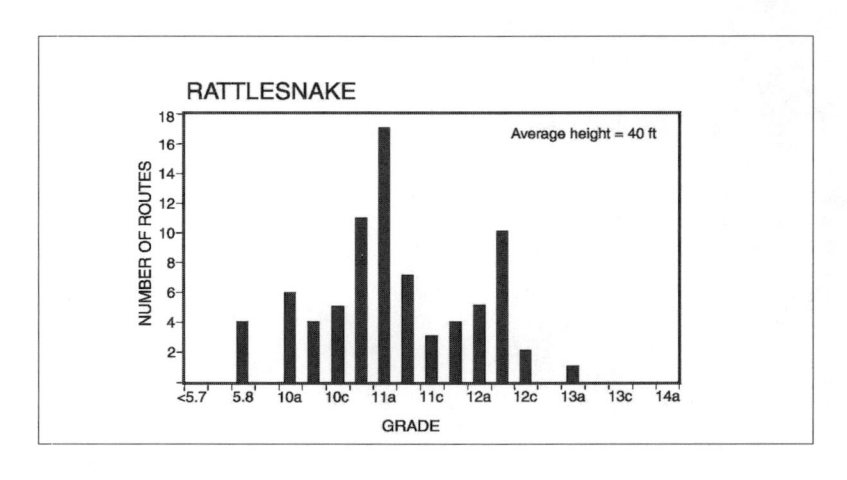

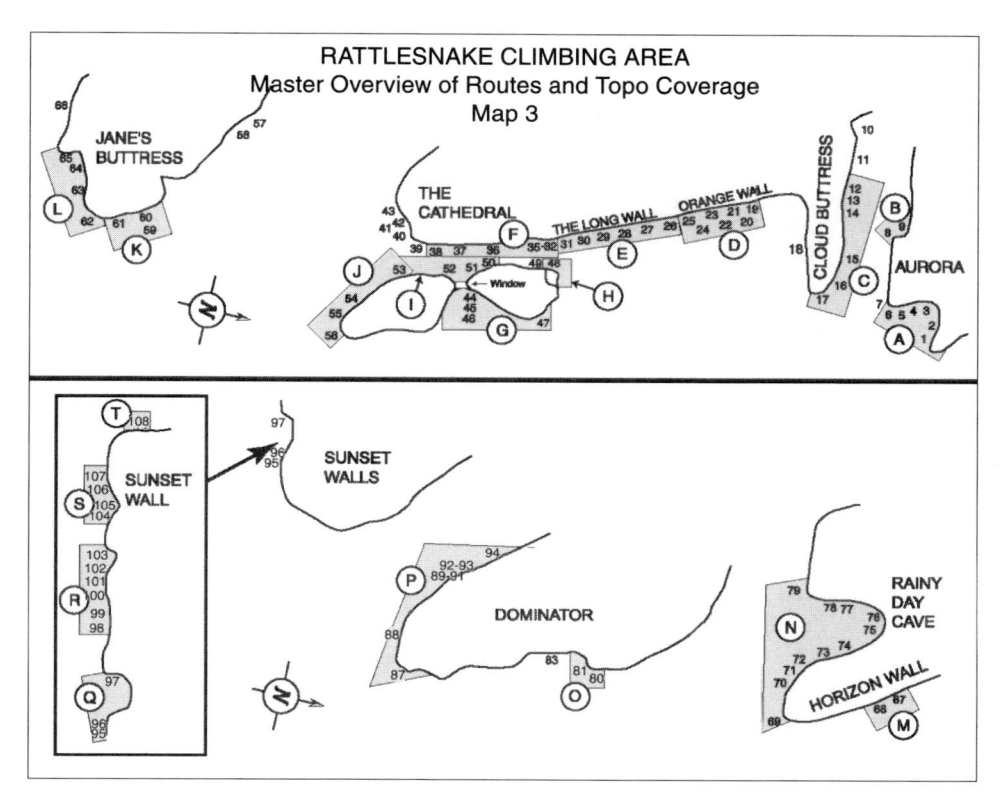

RATTLESNAKE CLIMBING AREA
Master Overview of Routes and Topo Coverage
Map 3

Raptor Nesting Closure

The Mushroom Towers, north of the Aurora Buttress, have a nesting closure (January until 2 weeks after the young have fledged). For more information contact the U.S. Fish and Wildlife Service.

Route Descriptions

Rattlesnake is known for its challenging climbs. With over one hundred routes established or in progress, it is the largest sport climbing area in Southwest Oregon. Climbs range from 25 to 90 feet in height with an overall average height of 40 feet. Over half of these climbs are rated 5.10d or higher. There is loose rock on some of the routes, so helmets are recommended. Most of the routes at Rattlesnake do not top out. Setting up a toprope often requires rappelling to top anchors. On some routes, stick-clipping the first bolt is recommended.

Many of Rattlesnake's overhanging and south facing cliffs remain climbable throughout most of the winter. It is also common to find these walls basking in sun while the Rogue, Umpqua, and Willamette Valleys remain blanketed by fog.

Aurora Buttress

(Topo A, B)

Approaching from the lower trail, the first formation will be the Aurora Buttress. The routes on this wall average 65 feet. Top ropes can only be established by rappelling from above.

1
Thumper
***5.10c

One crux move, the rest not so hard, but continually requiring thought. The first ascent was made using only pro. The lower portion has been bolted. The crux is located between the second and third bolts. A 0.75 Camalot works well for protecting this section. The top needs cams a bit bigger. FA Joe Chaves.

2
Aurora
***5.10d/11a

Great sustained face moves, sometimes thin, but always positive. Kind of long, a little technical, definitely good. Do not get sucked right at the start into flaky rock. Lay-back the ear. FA Bill NewComb.

2a
Borealis
***5.11d/5.12a

Left of *Aurora*. This route climbs a cool line up a chimney/dihedral, then cross over right (crux) and up an arete. FA Jerry Messinger, 2001.

3a,b
2001 :a Choss Odyssey Projects

Various projects

4
Project

Go up a loose scooped out area to a solid, clean crack. Take small cams and nuts for most of it, only the start will be bolted.

5
Broken Brain
***5.11a

The holds are solid, but not overly obvious. Crux is on lower portion of the route. The upper part is really solid.
FA Joe Chaves and Jerry Messinger.

6
Little Lucy
***5.11a

A neat series of moves with good holds and rock. A good introductory 5.11 climb.
FA Jerry Messinger and Bill NewComb.

Aurora Buttress
Topo A

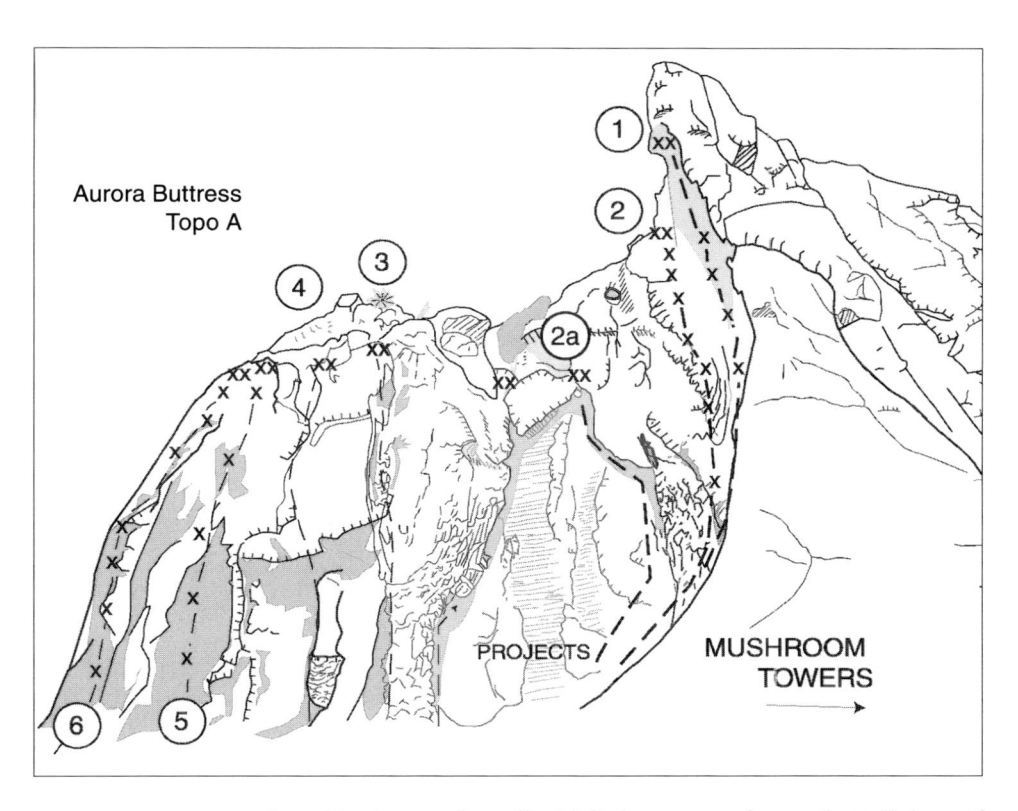

	7 Lady of Dreams Project	A cool jug low on the wall with little to grasp afterwards. Pull the roof and it's a cruise. Short but good for face slab pulling.
	8 The Ocelot **5.10d	Sustained 5.10c. Short but good for thin finger pulls. Easily toproped. FA Jerry Messinger and Bill NewComb.
	9 Uppyer Crack **5.9	A short gear protected crack with clean jams and solid placements. Take cams to 3 or 4 inches. Starts on the pad on the uphill left side of the buttress by a very big and old leaning snag. Perhaps one of the few and better crack climbs around. The only pure gear lead here in fact, but it still has face move possibilities. This is an excellent route for learning jam techniques. FA Jerry Messinger and Bill NewComb.

Rogue

128   Rattlesnake

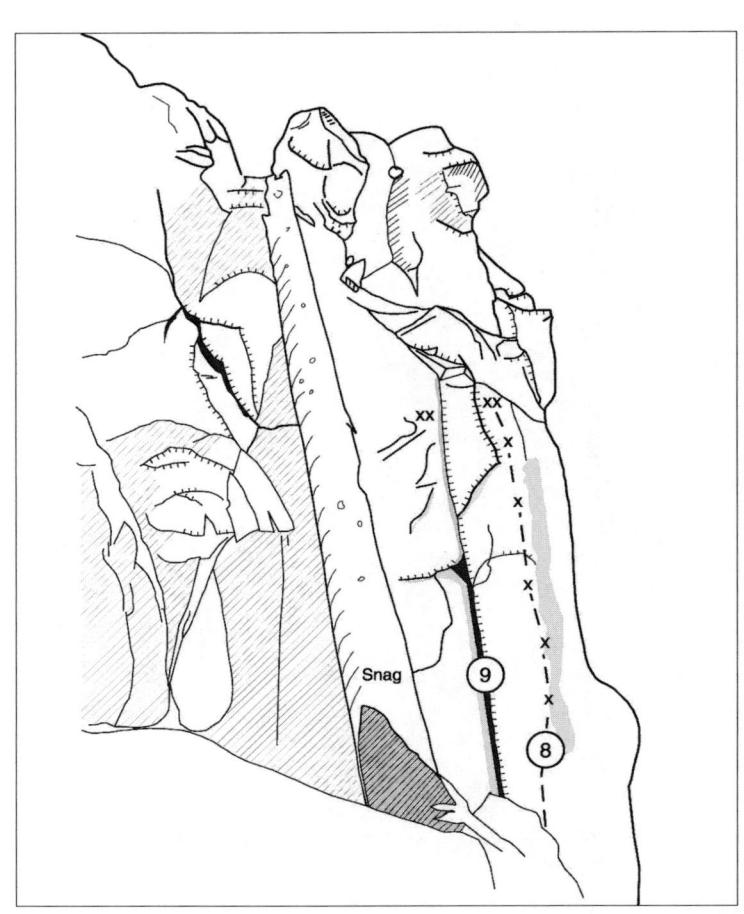

Aurora Buttress
Topo B

Snag   ⑨   ⑧

CLOUD BUTTRESS
(Topo C)
This prominent buttress has several good routes and a couple of boulder problems worth checking out.

10
Look Ma No Hands
V0-
Do the low angled slab with no hands, knees, or elbows. Good friction and footwork trainer. Down climb it too! Makes a good beginners footwork slab with hands, at V0-. Also provides access to the top of the Cloud Buttress for setting up the top ropes, or enjoy great views.

Rattlesnake   129

11
Karma Police
V1/V2

A good boulder problem that starts just up from the top ropes at some "fin" features. Start at the "fins" and pull-over. It has a fun lay-back to a crux reach and then becomes easier. FA Jerry Messinger and Jim Davis.

12
Rock Dancer
5.11 (TR)

The next three are short top ropes up the hill from *Soundtracker*. Each has it's own anchor.

13
Boomer
5.10 (TR)

Tricky pockets. Be careful setting up a top rope.

14
Shasta
5.8 (TR)

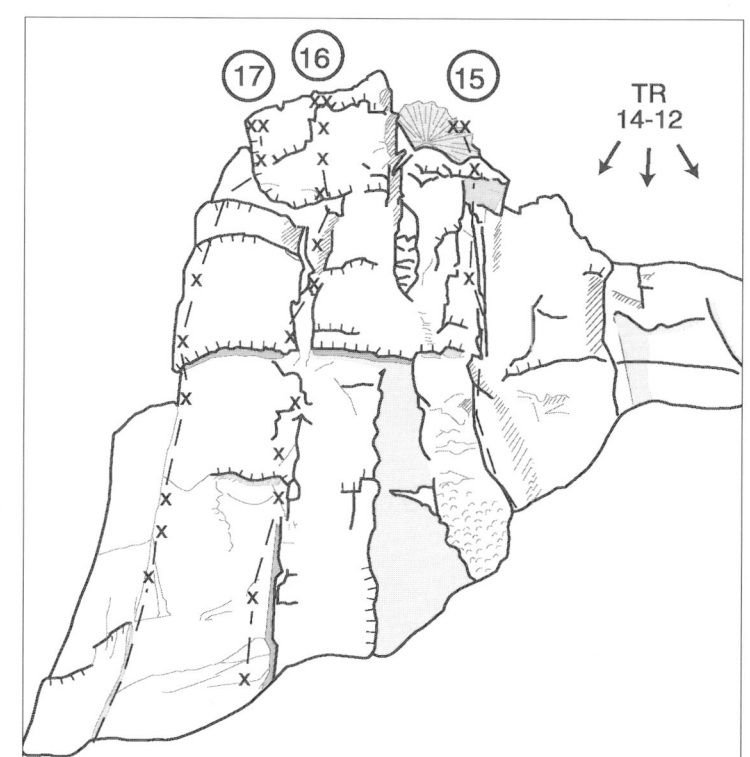

Cloud Buttress
Topo C

Rogue

15 Soundtracker **5.10a	This is a popular route. Climb the face and slots to a little roof at the end. Fun and solid moves up a nice line. Use caution if setting up a top rope without leading the route. Good forest views. FA Bill NewComb.	
16 The Great Bear **5.10d	The rock sounds hollow but the quality is good. The crux is near the ever steepening top. FA Bill NewComb.	
17 Cloud Drifter **5.11c	A beautiful line on the end of the buttress. The rock isn't perfect but the technical moves will make you float. FA Joe Chaves.	
18 Butt Bar Express **5.10b	Stay along the bolt line, it's easier to the right but will lead you astray. Using the tree not allowed! A decent face climb. FA. Bill NewComb	

ORANGE WALL

(Topo D)

The lines aren't bad on the Orange Wall and it's steeper than it looks. Recent development has sandwiched routes in as close as you'd ever want. The rock quality ranges from really good to pretty bad. The routes are all fairly difficult. After the original route, Whistler, the others names have followed a beverage theme.

20 Orange Crush 5.12b, Ac	Some four star climbing on the upper part is unfortunately carved out of some of the worst rock at Rattlesnake. This route may not last long, in it's original state, but the moves are excellent with cool steep jugs in the middle.	
21 Surge Project	Hard, mid 13's at least.	
22 Red Bull 12b/c ?, Ac	May have received a first ascent in 1999. No Information.	

Climber on
Thumper (5.10b)
Jerry Messinger

23   Sustained with thin cranks on great rock, deceptively steep.
Jolt
5.12d ?, Ac

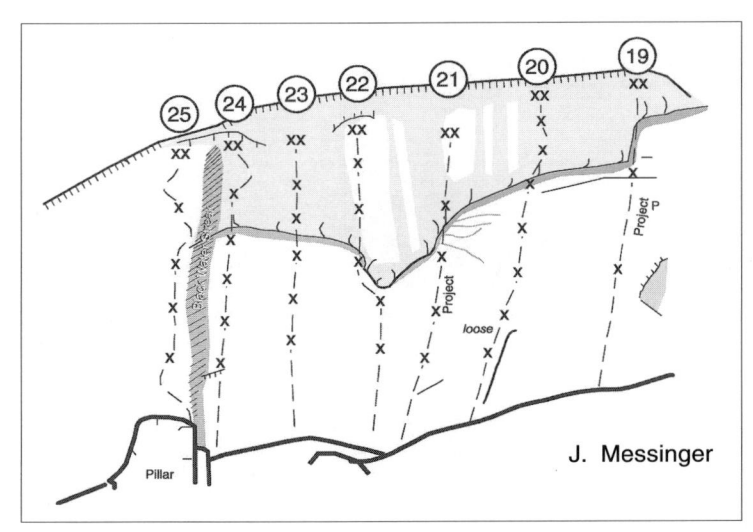

The Orange Wall
Topo D

J. Messinger

24
Whistler
***5.11c
One of the first routes done at Rattlesnake. Climb up the black water streak into a depression and pull a tricky crux onto a ledge to the right, just before the end. FA Jerry Messinger.

25
Sunny Delight
**5.11b
On the shallow prow right of *Schizophrenia*, straightforward moves up the face and edges.
FA Cory Jones.

LONG WALL
(Topo E)
The Long Wall includes the Orange Wall and continues to the Cathedral. These routes have some fairly long lines, with varying rock quality. The Farther north, the more they ledge out in the middle, making for routes that are close to two pitches. These routes top out at the first crest, while the climbing is still good.

26
Schizophrenia
**5.11a
Up a groove to the right of *The Dagger*, this route is decent although shorter people may find it harder.
FA Joe Chaves

27a
The Dagger
***5.11a
Climb the rib starting at the boulder. The big ledge above causes too much drag so the anchor is placed at that point. Excellent route.
FA Jerry Messinger.

27b Heart of Darkness Project — Start up a low ledge from where a boulder came off. Continue to the upper head wall using small strenuous holds. Good luck!

28 Topaz **5.11b — Go either left (5.11a) of right (5.11b) up this route. The right has a long reach move (tough if your short) and great holds. Avoid the ledge left near the finish staying on the gray rock. Tricky at the end. The left finish is similar to the right but a little easier. Both start on less than perfect rock but the upper parts are great. FA Jerry Messinger/Bill NewComb.

29 Woman in the Mist **5.11a — Climb the dihedral, with a single hard move. The rest is relatively easy, but hard enough and sustained so as to make it interesting and fun. Good stone. FA Joe Chaves.

30 Rufous **5.12a — Good climb until the route reaches the slab. The pockets and micro holds are not as fun, but challenging. Good rock quality. FA Bill NewComb.

Cory Jones leading the cruxy moves of Sunny Delight (5.11b), Orange Wall. Jerry Messinger

Rogue

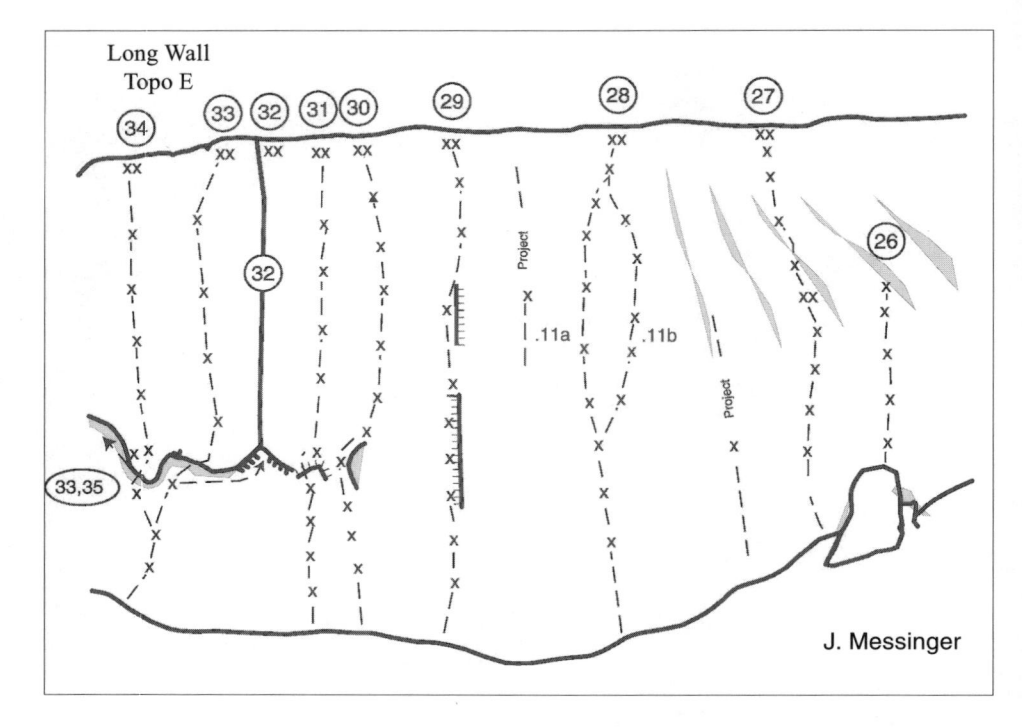

Rattlesnake

Long Wall Topo E

J. Messinger

31 Little Fatty **5.12a/b	Long and technical. The crux is in the middle pulling over the big roof. This is a good climb despite hollow rock down low. The top is solid, and the bolts are good. FA Cory Jones.

THE CATHEDRAL

(Topos F-J)

This is the showcase crag at Rattlesnake. The cathedral is a spectacular formation. It is shady in the summer, gets some midday sun in the winter, and is dry in the rain, unless it rains a lot, then it can seep. These routes are some of the most spectacular, ranging from 5.10 to 5.13. Most are steeper than they look. The crag is divided into the "main cliff", the "window wall", and the "outside window wall". Laps and circuits are common training material here.

32 Iceman ***5.11a	Same start as *Girl with Flaxen Hair*. The route goes up the clean crack on the right after the rest. Take pro to 3 inches. The crux is a mantle at the scoop near the top. A tiny foot ledge out right helps. Slippery when wet. FA Jerry Messinger.

Jerry Messinger climbing inside Rainy Day Cave. Greg Orton

**33
Girl with
Flaxen Hair
****5.12b**
Spectacular line up an overhanging head wall. Totally classic. Common start with *Iceman*, clip the right "third" bolt, pull around to a rest, clipping the second head wall bolt from the right before going back, down, and onto the thing by stepping across left with tricky moves. FA Cory Jones.

**34
The Tonsil
Project (5.12+)**
Shares common start with routes 31-35. From the third bolt, clip the first "tonsil" bolt, then unclip the third to reduce rope drag. This is one of Rattlesnake's steepest routes yet and the cranks are difficult. It is OK to stem near the end; do not hit your backside if you fall there, but the hard part is below by then.

Rattlesnake

35
Rattlesnake Reality
****5.12a/b

Another one of those roof cracks. Start at the common with routes 31-35. Climb from belay ledge up 2 bolts, then clip the furthest left of the two "third" bolts. Follow the horizontal roof crack with a couple jams, but mostly stems and sport moves. Three cams should suffice in bomber placements; 0.5, .75, and #1 Camalots were used on the first ascent. Clip the 3rd bolt on Pandemonium, the 4th of Full Circle, and head for the Psych anchor, clipping one more on the way. Long draw on Full Circle bolt will help reduce the rope drag. A full body and cardiac workout. FA Jerry Messinger

36
Pandemoniun Project

Project probably low 13 range. Start on a deceptive pillar, and pull the radically steep roof to the top of the Cathedral. Same anchor as #38. This will be four stars.

37
Full Circle
****5.12a

Power lay-backs up an offset, solid rock, with jugs and jams at the end. Tricky kneebars and other creative moves will help. The first ascent was made onsight. Steep and stellar. The start frustrates many. Most stick clip the second bolt. FA Joe Chaves/ Jerry Messinger

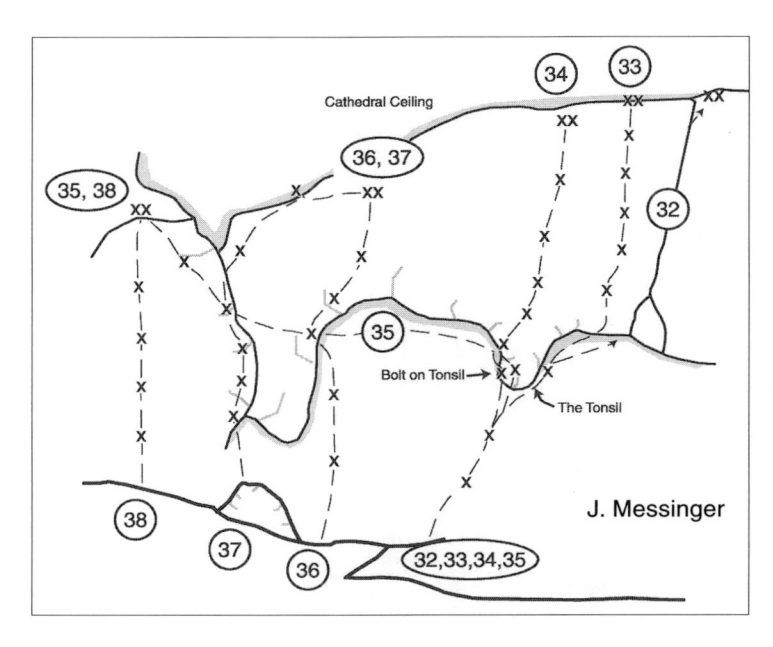

Cathedral Topo F

38
Psychadelicatessen
****5.12b/c

The first steep and modern bouldery route that motivated Jerry to developing the Cathedral. From the top of this route is where good holds inside the formation were first recognized. This route was therefore somewhat of a catalyst. Its sustained bouldery moves, not especially hard, are totally classic. FA Jerry Messinger.

39
Barney
**5.9

Climb up the right side of the big "slot" with good small cams or nuts, plus a few bolts. Finish right, then reach out left to clip the anchor chains. FA Jerry Messinger.

> THERE'S A PLACE IN EVERY SOUL WHERE TECHNOLOGY WILL NEVER GO.

Photo: Jerry Messinger

40
Beavis Buddies
**5.11a

Climb up the left side of the slot and skirt left on the roof. Really good for a slabby and footwork oriented route. You never really strain or get pumped, but it's still 11a. Good training route where smooth moves rule. Look for Beavis from the belay! FA Joe Chaves and Jerry Messinger.

Rogue

Rattlesnake

41
Birthday Bash
**5.10c/d

Start at the bottom of the "slot" and go left to a ledge. Rack your draws on the right hip. Climb left side of boltline. Weird, but good moves to the left. Climb up the arete and left of it in spots. There is little rope drag. FA Jerry Messinger.

42
***5.10c/d
New Years Day

To make this route challenging, avoid stemming left at the start, and climb up these bouldery moves past the third bolt to an easier slab above. Great rock with tricky moves. FA Jim Davis.

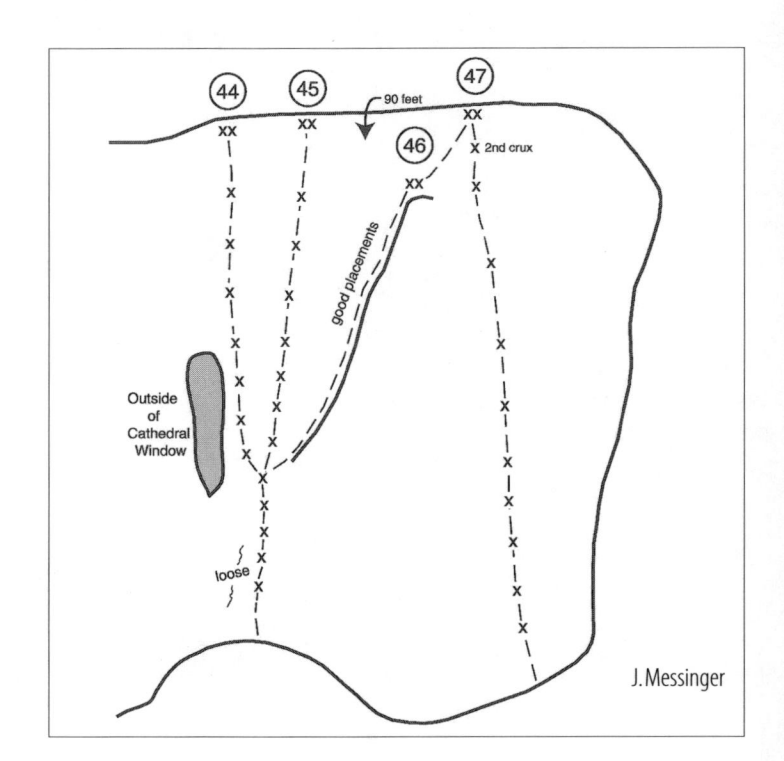

Outside the Window
Topo G

J. Messinger

OUTSIDE THE WINDOW
(Topo G, *Maps 2, 3*)
These four routes are all long, with loose starts low and great moves up high.

44
Angela
**5.11d
Same start as #45/46, but take the left exit and pull off the side of the window through a tricky crux and finish on great pockets. Named in remembrance of a friend. FA Joe Chaves.

45
Bird of Prey
**5.10d
The loose start gives way to great pockets on cool rock. One of the early routes, it is a little over bolted perhaps. Bring many draws to clip all the bolts. FA Bill NewComb.

46
Mountain Lion's Perch
**5.10a
Routes #44-46 share a common start below and outside of the window. *Mountain Lion's Perch* breaks right and follows a crack to a ledge. Take pro for the crack.
FA Bill NewComb.

47
Secret Forest
**5.11a/b
A 50 meter rope is almost too short, so use caution. A good rest in the middle precedes the first crux section, followed by easier climbing to near the end then another crux section that is very good. FA Jerry Messinger.

WINDOW WALL
(Topos H-J, *Maps 2, 3*)
Inside the Cathedral opposite the main cliff is a large obvious window. This window frames a killer view and a few good routes. Window wall extends all the way down the hill to Fluff's route, outside the actual arch. More fun than you can ever imagine.

48
Leisure Days
***5.12b
A little loose low, but above the ledge it is solid and the arching flare is great and pumping. The crux is through the roof at the end. A great line which helped inspire much of what has been developed here today.
FA Jerry Messinger.

49
Amy
****5.13a
One of the hardest routes in Southern Oregon. Great rock with 60 feet of steep and technical cranking, awesome moves, and a phenomenal line on the right side of the arete. Several have commented that this is the best line in this part of Oregon. The arete is used more as you get higher. Beautiful rock. FA Jerry Messinger.

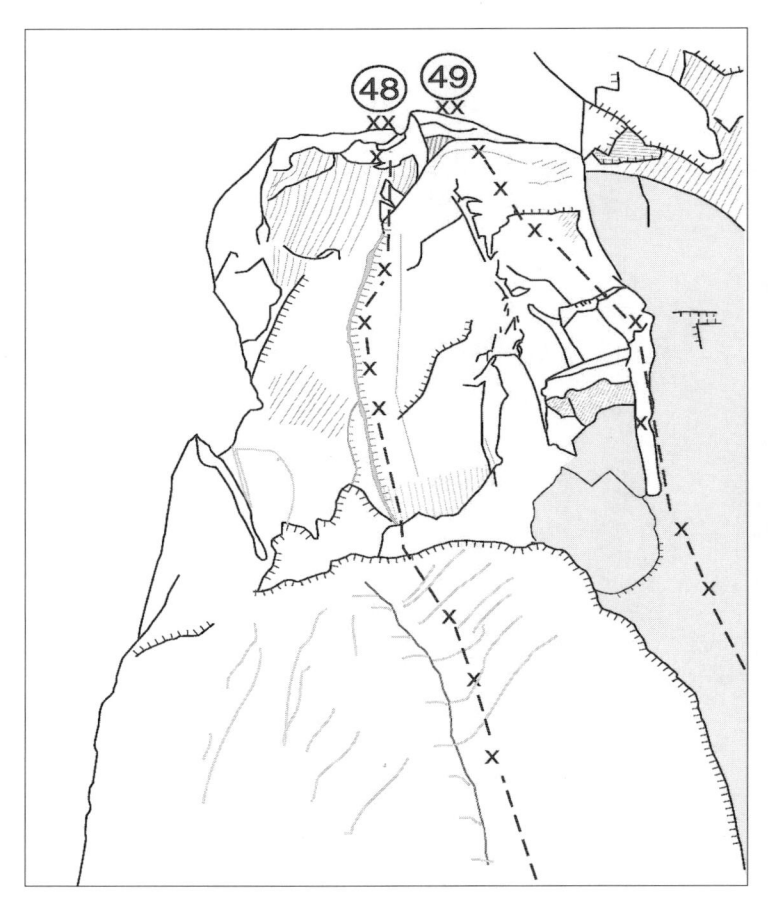

Window Wall
Topo H

50
Ikenseaor Crack
***5.11d**

Fun moves up a very thin seam, with a wild dynamic "seam splitting stem" crux at the end.
FA Jerry Messinger.

51
The Groove
***5.12a**

Classic small pockets on great rock to the window seat anchor below the roof. Popular and easy to top rope after warming up on the *Window Seat*. If you do, clip into the fifth bolt on *Window Seat* as a directional.
FA Cory Jones.

52
Window Seat
***5.11a**

From the right of the window, stick clip the first bolt. Climb up the flare with a tricky crux at the fourth bolt. The fifth bolt is not part of the original redpoint but keeps a follower from a large swing if they fall at the crux. FA Jerry Messinger.

Rattlesnaske 141

53
Arabesque
****5.10a

The classic warm-up route with big yet hard to read holds. Start down and to the right. Many people try to go off the belay ledge and stay too far left. Get around to the pods low on the wall. At the midway ledge, the route stays left and straight up, mostly on good but sometimes hidden holds. FA Bill NewComb.

54
Indigo
**5.10d

Cruxy low on the wall. *Indigo* starts thin then easing off-with good moves and solid stone to the top. Tricky clips low.
FA Bill NewComb.

The Window Wall
Topo i

Rogue

142 Rattlesnake

55
The Shadow
**5.11b

Small holds, a bit contrived perhaps, stay left a little. Keep going to the top on one of the other routes if you want a long climb.
FA Bill NewComb.

56
Fluff's Route
**5.10b

Starts on the lower end of the buttress and up the edge. The crux is at the start, with easy climbing to the top and then a hard move there too. FA Bill NewComb.

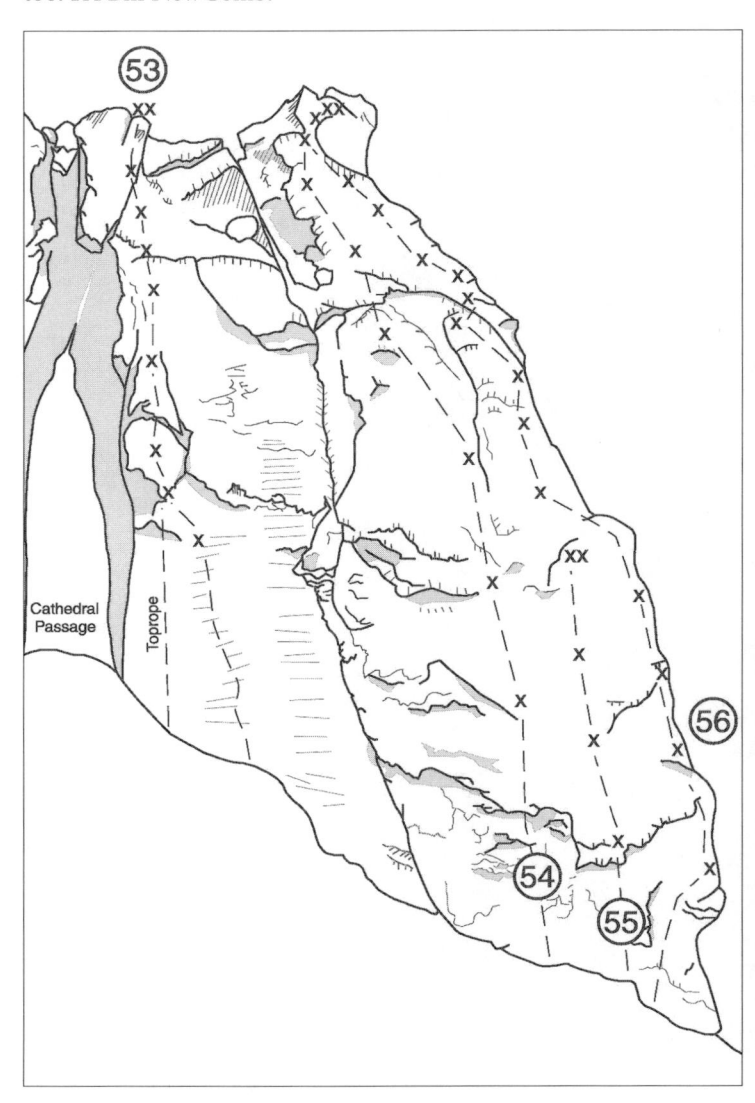

The Window Wall
Topo J

JANE'S BUTTRESS

(Topos K and L, *Maps 2, 3*)
Uphill on either end the routes are short. Routes on the low point of the buttress are close to 75 feet long.

57 Jimmy's 5.8 Project (possibly 5.13+)	A tough slab with very few features. Still needs bolting.
58 Not Forgotten **5.12a/b	Clean rock with hard sustained moves. Bouldery and a classic climb if it were longer. As a scary boulder problem it would be 4 stars, and 44 more for fear. FA Jerry Messinger.
59 Split Decision ***5.10a	Fun, easy jugs with a crux on brown varnish. Small but positive holds and thin foot placements. You have the option to split left for the hard (5.10a) finish, or end by climbing straight up to the right (5.9). A good warm up if you do 5.11 or harder. FA Jim Davis.
60 Mirror Image **5.11c	Shares the first 60 feet with *Split Decision*. Break left from the belay ledge and continue for 3 more bolts to the top. Finish on a couple of the same holds used on *Shadow Caster*, but with the opposite hand. FA Jerry Messinger.
61 Shadow Caster ****5.11d	Start on weird blocks, with a technical crux low on the wall, then tricky climbing to a ledge, rest up, the finish is a classic and it's a pumper! From the ledge continue up and right. Over the top is a great hold to clip the top anchor with. Hint: Unclip the forth bolt after you clip the fifth, to cut drag. The rock to the right was not appropriate for bolting. FA Jerry Messinger
62 Lady in Red ***5.11b	A classic arete with mostly face moves on the right. There is a killer hold between two top anchor bolts. FA Jerry Messinger and Bill NewComb.

144   Rattlesnake

63
Charybdis
***5.12a

Charybdis is a route that starts on less than perfect rock until after the first bolt where it quickly gives way to good and unique features on a wall that is steeper than it looks. Some cool moves. FA Jerry Messinger.

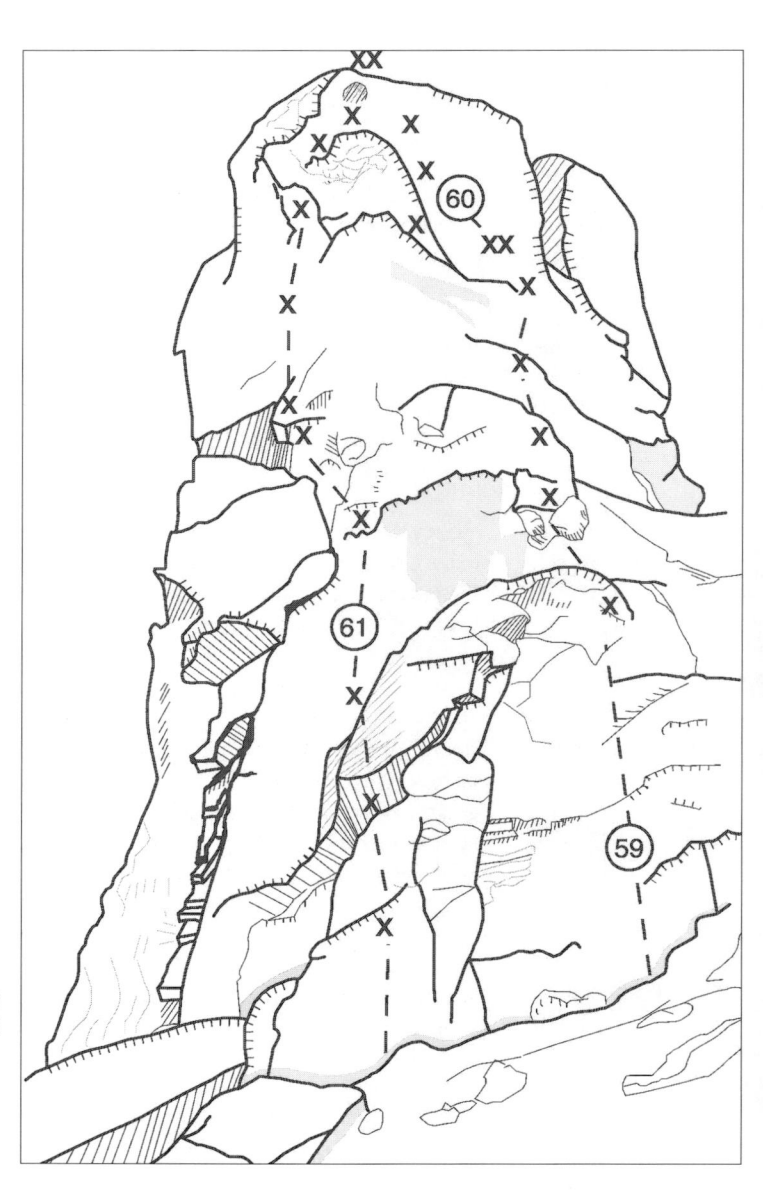

Jane's Buttres
Topo K

Wendy Schlep on Arebesque (5.10a)
Photo: Jerry Messinger

Rattlesnake

64
Ringer
**5.10b/c

Starts off the ledge right of a little cave. *Ringer* has sustained moves on a steepening wall with a distinct crux pulling over the lip. Good rock and fun moves. FA Jerry Messinger and Bill NewComb.

65
Bat Flight Express
**5.11c

The rock is solid at least, but the moves are tweaky. FA Jerry Messinger and Joe Chaves.

66
Janeivour
**5.8

Very short but the moves are good, the rock is solid. FA Bill NewComb.

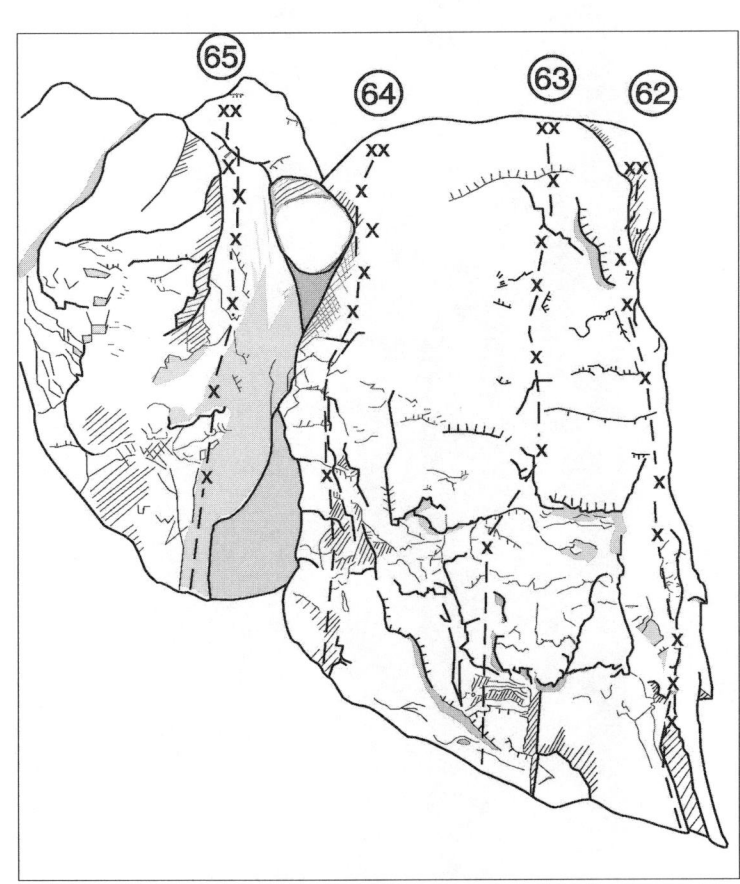

Jane's Buttress
Topo L

Rattlesnaske 147

Jerry Messinger climing In Oregon We Rust (5.10d). Greg Orton

Rogue

HORIZON WALL

(Topo M and N, *Maps 2, 3*)
The start of Horizon Wall is a good line. Horizon Air is on the corner arete of the buttress below the Rainy Day cave. Horizon Wall extends all the way up towards Janivour, the last route on Jane's Buttress.

67
Afterburner
***5.12b
Right of the tree, sustained cranks on steep, clean, solid rock. There is a good left-hand hold up over the top at the end.
FA Jerry Messinger.

68
Lost Horizon
**5.11c/d
Just left of the leaning tree, tricky but not a hard start, then technical with cranking little pockets. Too bad the top part isn't fifty feet more of the same. FA Jerry Messinger.

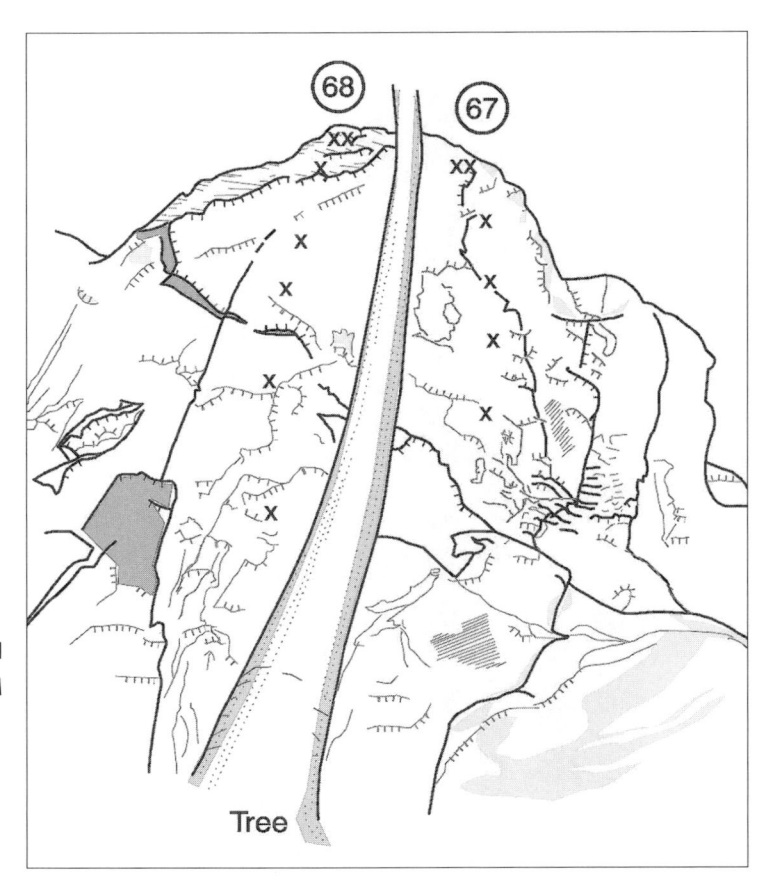

Horizon Wall
Topo M

RAINY DAY CAVE

(Topo N, *Maps 2, 3*)
A popular hangout when it's wet, and also when it's hot. Short but sweet routes with an element of steepness. Watch the back of your head as you near the top of some of these routes, especially if you fall! A helmet is definitely recommended when climbing in the Cave.

69
Horizon Air
**5.11a

Horizon Air climbs up the arete, starting from the belay pad. Climb to the right side for a bit, moving left and straight up after that. Joins and finishes the same as *Misty Horizon*. Cool pockets at the crux. FA Jerry Messinger.

70
Misty Horizon
**5.10d

This is a technical route with entertaining moves. The rock is pretty solid, despite how some of it may look. May deserve more than two stars because of its uniqueness. FA Jerry Messinger.

71
Rain Man
***5.10d/5.11a

Rain Man is an excellent sustained route, with cool jugs to finish on. Top roping might be difficult due to rope drag. FA Jim Davis.

72
Cloudburst
**5.11a

First route outside the cave, just right of the tree. Belay at the top of the steps. A definite crux at the second bolt with a tricky finish. The rocks a little loose as you start, but becomes better as you climb.
FA Jim Davis and Joe Chaves.

73
In Oregon We Rust
***5.10c/d

Steep wall with good holds. Start up and to your left on the "ledge" then go around the corner to the right and up. The second clip is tricky but it offered the best bolt placement. Cool lay-backs mark the finish. Popular and good for laps. FA Jerry Messinger.

74
Welcome to Oregon
***5.12b

This is the middle route up the cave's back right wall. It has steep moves and a roof problem. Solid rock and great moves, with a wicked pull at the lip. "Pinching E.T.'s throat with the right hand is how to clip the anchor." Grabbing the draws is off route. FA Jerry Messinger.

75
Rain Sucks
**5.10a

Rain Sucks offers a variety of moves packed into a short but nice climb: stems, thin, and steep with jugs at the top. Shares the top anchors with *Chinese Water Torture*. FA Jerry Messinger.

Rogue

Rattlesnake

76
Chinese Water Torture
**5.10a

Short but sweet, the left of two routes at the back of the cave. Try the sit down starts, traverse in from as far right as you want for a warm-up route. FA Jerry Messinger.

77
Galoshes
**5.12b/c

Galoshes has the same start as *Water Buffalo* for two bolts, then breaks to the right and up. There is a stem on the last move. Cool moves. FA Jerry Messinger.

78
Water Buffalo
project

The last route inside the cave on the left wall, three bolts straight up. Just a boulder problem really, and probably at least 5.13.

79
Frozen
***5.11a

Just outside the cave on the left, along the arete. Cool moves with less than obvious holds on white rock.
FA Jim Davis.

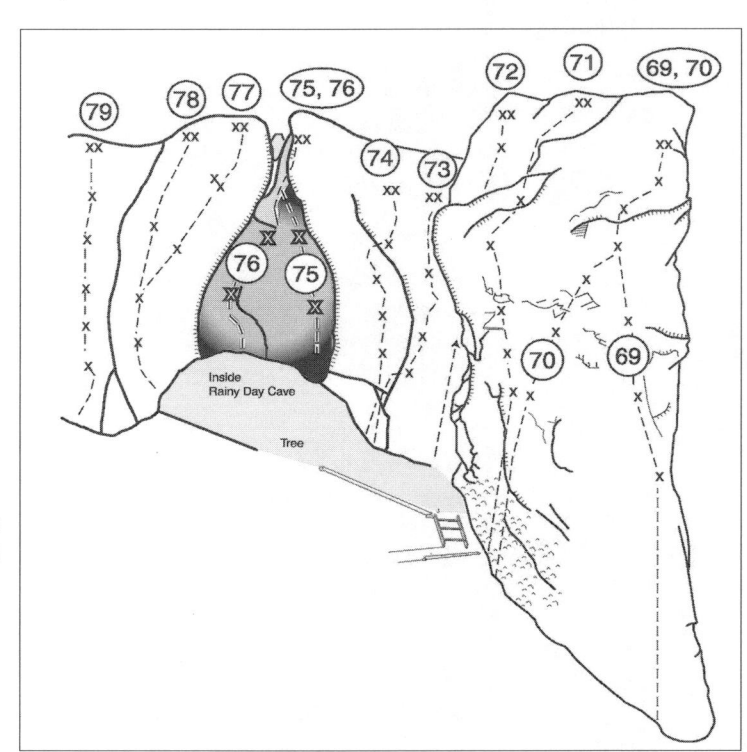

Rainy Day Cave
Topo N

Rattlesnaske 151

"[Climbing] teaches us to discover the transcendental core of our own selves in an immediate and practical sense, to 'taste' divine being in the here-and now."
— *Karlfried Graf Durckheim*

Jerry Messinger clipping into the third hanger on Welcome to Oregon (5.12b), Rainy Day Cave. Greg Orton

DOMINATOR WALL

(Topo O, Maps 2, 3, 4)
Dominator is a 90 foot tall east facing wall. Routes range from 25 to 30 meters in length.

80 Black Swan **5.10d	A route worth making. Unfortunately less than perfect rock down low tarnishes what is a superb route up higher. 25 meters protected with 11 bolts. FA Jerry Messinger and Bill NewComb.

81 Flakes of Wrath Project	Possibly 5.13. Wildly double-overhanging arete.

82 Project	Long, bulging wall l right of Scorpion Arete.

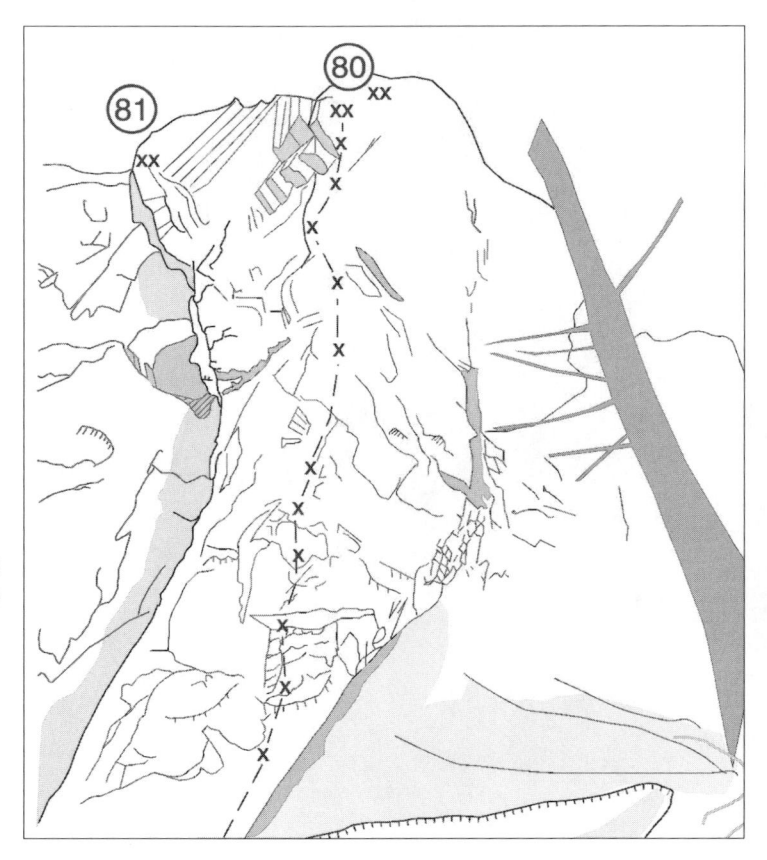

Dominator Wall
Topo O

Rattlesnaske 153

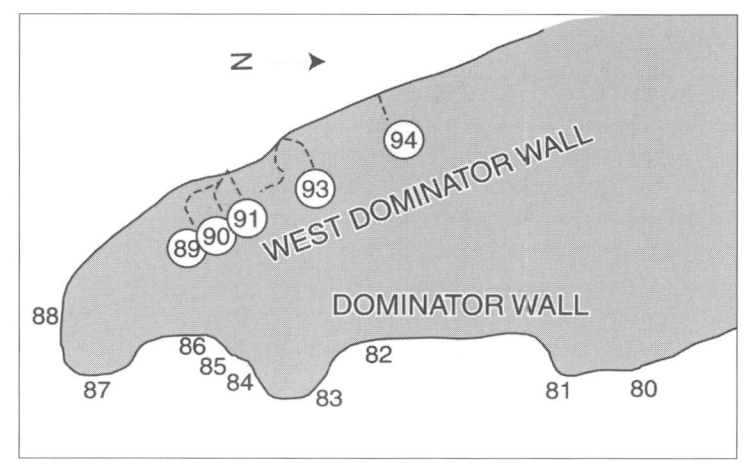

Map 4

| 83 Scorpion ****5.12a | Power crux up first bulge to a midway rest, then try not to pump-out on a spectacular overhanging arete up high. 60 meter rope recommended with note at the end of the belayer's side. 55 meters with 13 bolts. FA Jerry Messinger, March 2001. |

| 84 Flight of the Dead Souls ****5.10c | Like Scorpion it has a technical crux low on the route and a pumpy spectacular headwall finish above. 60 meters rope recommended. Protected with 12 bolts. |

| 85 Project | Begins on *Flight of the Dead Souls* and pulls the headwall then climbs to the left. At least a 60 meters will be needed to lower off. |

| 86 Dark Shadows **5.10a | After a forgettable start, stem all the way to the top using the long gully/chimney. 60 meters rope recommended. Protected with 13 bolts. FA Bill Newcomb, 2001. |

| 87 KaraKorum ***5.11a | A long pitch on rock that is much better than it looks from the bottom. Several intriguing cruxes split with good rests, and a pump 100 feet up. Protected with 12 bolts, 60 meter rope recommended. FA Bill Newcomb, 2001. |

Rogue

WEST DOMINATOR

(Topo P, Maps 2, 3, 4)
On the southwest side of the Dominator Walls the climbs become shorter as the hill climbs steeply between Dominator and the Sunset Walls. Climbs range from 40 to 90 feet in height. Much of the rock is fragile, and a few projects remain on the south buttress. Acquiring the patience to clean these is the crux. Several gems can be found on the west side in a section of clean rock. West Dominator becomes obvious as the trail switchbacks up the hill. It gets lots of sun in the winter and quickly dries to become climbable. Find the trail, do not scramble up the hillside.

88 This Ain't Area 51 Project	Climbs the end of buttress above steps.	
89 2 North **5.10c	Common start with *Comfortably Numb* and *Chain Saw Psyco Dork*. Traverse right towards tree after first bolt. Climb straight up at tree through thin technical moves. FA Joe Chaves and Jerry Messinger, 2000.	
90 Comfortably Numb ***5.11c	Common start with *2-North* and *Chain Saw Psyco Dork*. Traverse right after first bolt, and straight up between *2-North* and *Chain Saw Psyco Dork* after second bolt. Very cool moves on very cool rock. FA Jerry Messinger, 2001.	

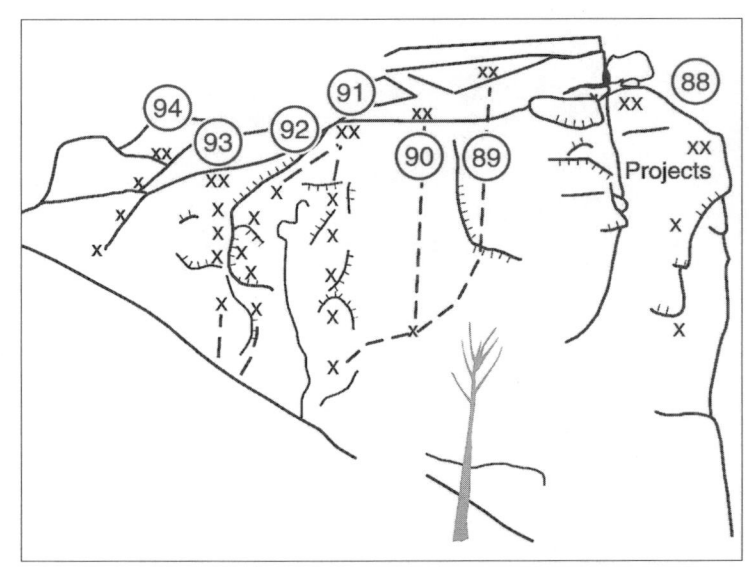

West Dominator
Topo P

Cory Jones on Split Decision, 5.10a. Jerry Messinger

Rattlesnake

91
Chainsaw
Psycho Dork
****5.11b

Common start with *2-North* and *Comfortably Numb*. A bit loose at the very start, then solid, steep and extremely fun with cool moves. There are big holds, a small but positive crux, then a lay-back with a jug fest to the top. Don't miss this one. 5 bolts+ anchor. FA Jerry Messinger.

92
Captain Quaalude
***5.12a

Steep and sustained to a boulder problem move, then jugs arching right to the same anchor as *Chainsaw Psyco Dork*. Fun and solid after some minor looseness at the very start. 5 bolts+ anchor. FA Jerry Messinger or possibly an unknown climber from Ashland.

93
Master Hwang
**5.11a

Master Hwang (pronounced "fong," Korean) Cross tricky face to little roof, then up the dihedral. Often wet during rainy season, but routes next to it are always dry. 4 bolts+ anchor. FA Joe Chaves.

94
Carson Hall
**5.10b

Fun laybaking lead with straight forward finish above. 3 bolts and chain. FA Jerry Messinger, 2000.

SUNSET WALL

(Topos Q-U, Maps 2, 3)

The southwestern most crags at Rattlesnake provide good climbing in the winter during sunny weather. Don't be fooled by fog in the Rogue Valley and western Oregon lowlands. In the winter Rattlesnake is usually sunny and 60 degrees at the sunset walls. So, bring shorts in late December and early January. Early morning will find these routes shaded in the summer, and of course spring and fall is always great unless it's a classic Oregon downpour. These crags overlook the Cabin Creek drainage, and the view is nice as are the trees. On top, at the south end of the plateau trail, you can see Mt. Shasta and Mt. McLaughlin in the snow capped Cascade Range.

95
The Bolted Barbie
**5.10b

There is a large tree close by. Early winter sun. 4 bolts+ anchor. FA a group of Corvallis climbers, names unknown.

96
Science Barbie
**5.6

Route left of the large tree. Originally climbed using gear only. This route has a variety of moves and receives early winter sun. 4 bolts+ anchor. FA Emma Coddington.

"When the mind is nowhere it is everywhere.
When it occupies 1/10 it is absent in 9/10."
— *Takvan*

Justin leading right on Split Decision (5.9) on Jane's Buttres. Jerry Messinger

Rattlesnake

Sunset Wall Area
Topo Q

97
East Berlin
**5.10d

Tricky moves, gets early sun in the winter. FA Jerry Messinger

98
Pleasure Victim
****5.12b/c

A stellar roof problem with killer moves! Shares the first bolt with The *Metro* then go straight up. 3 bolts+ anchor. FA Jerry Messinger.

99
The Metro
****5.11a

One of the best roof routes around. Awesome moves pull the big roof, but technique will get you further. Not super long, but a must do! Shares first Bolt with *Pleasure Victim* then goes left and up. 4 bolts+ anchor. FA Joe Chaves

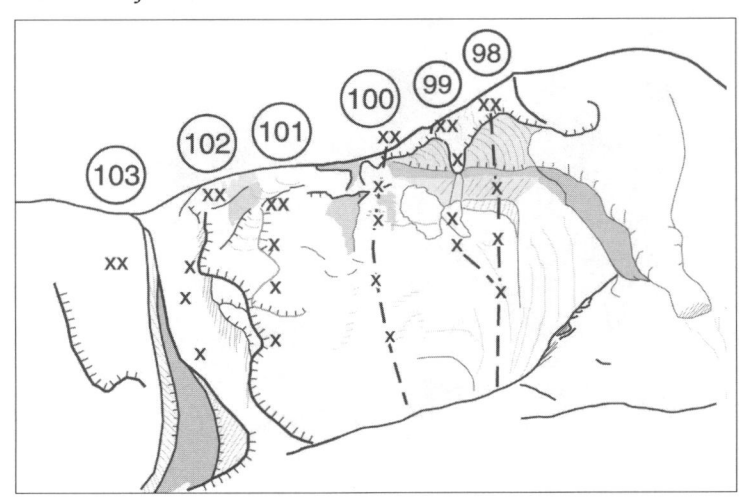

Sunset Wall Area
Topo R

100 Airlift 5.10b-5.11a	A nice line up the gray streak to a difficult roof problem above. This route is to the left of *Metro*. Named *Airlift* because you may need one to pull the roof. If you do the roof before calling it quits, it adds a 5.11 dyno. 30 feet with 4 bolts. FA Jerry Messinger and Jim Davis, 2001.
101 Blockade **5.10a/b	Loose at the very start, then solid, with good tricky moves. 3 bolts+anchor. FA Jerry Messinger.
102 West Berlin **5.10d/11a	Right side of the little cave. 3 bolts + anchor. FA Jerry Messinger.

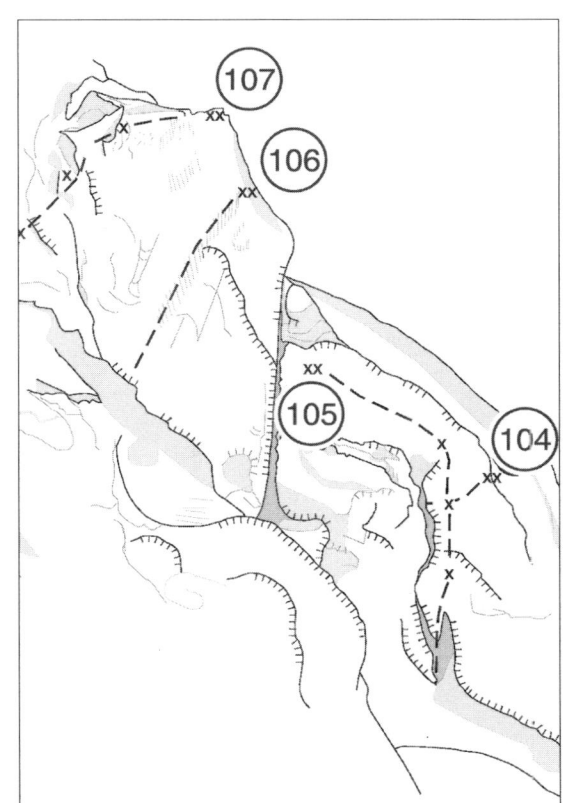

Sunset Wall Area
Topo S

Rogue

103
Gray Matter
5.10a
Left side of the little cave marks the end of the Berlin Wall. Climbing is on technical edges of good quality rock. FA Mark Ivers and Jerry Messinger, May 2003.

104
Chowder
**5.10c
Face climb to the right side of the bolt line, clipping on the left. 2 bolts+ anchor.
FA Jerry Messinger.

105
The Clam
**5.8
Climb the right edge of the clam, clipping 3 bolts to the right, then move left across the top of the clam. 3 bolts+ anchor.
FA Jerry Messinger.

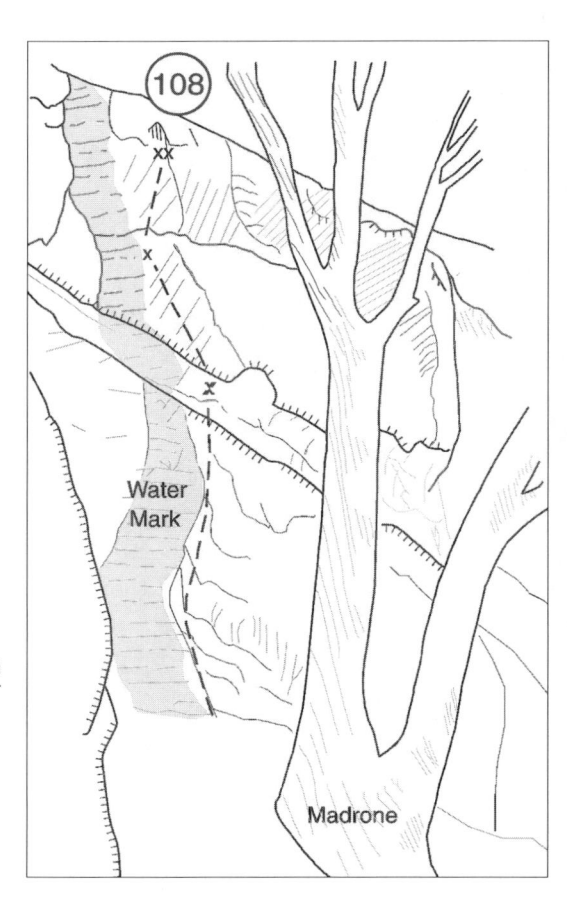

Sunset Wall Area
Topo T

Rattlesnaske

106
TR Problem
5.12+
Climb shallow groove on micro-holds with clean rock, it is just hard!

107
Sunset Arete
***5.11a
Nice moves up a clean arete. It's good and tricky. There are some balance moves at the very end as you move from the right to the left side of the arete. 4 bolts+ anchor. FA Jerry Messinger.

108
Red Sky
**5.12a/b
Short bouldery route, on the far west end of the area, in the gully that connects to the top trail. 2 bolts+ anchor.
FA Jerry Messinger.

109
I Peter 2:7 & 8
***5.10c/d or V0+
The crux is down low, but the finish still requires attention. 1 bolt.
FA Jerry Messinger and Mark Ivers, 2003.

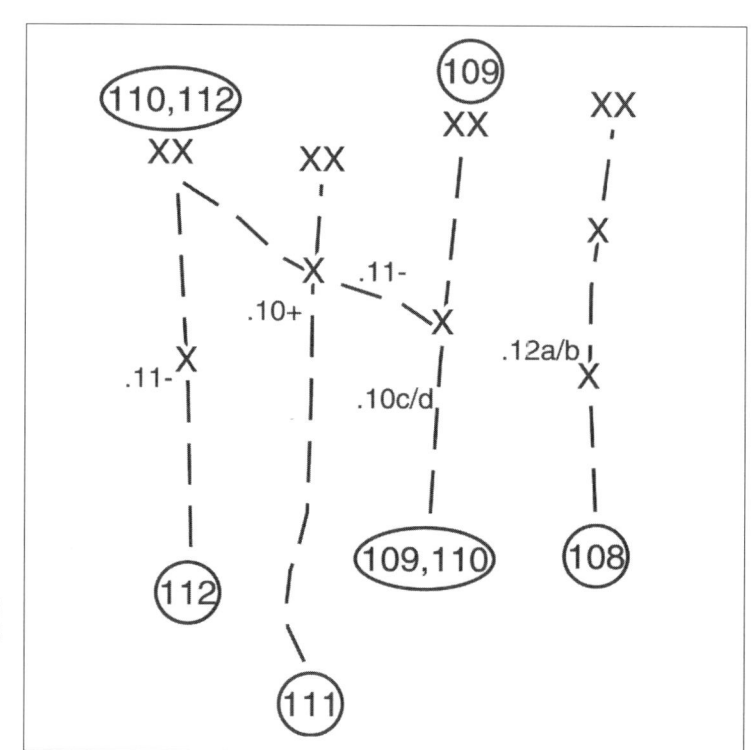

Sunset Wall Area
Topo U

Rogue

110 I Psalm 89:26 **5.11- or V1		Same start as *I Peter*. Climb left after first bolt, make a funky move then clip the next bolt. Same finish as *I Kings*. FA Jerry Messinger, 2003.

111 Isaiah 2:21 **5.10+ TR		A toprope squeeze in between *I Psalm* and *I Kings* using the second bolt of *I Psalm* as a directional. Focus on sidepull and go for the pocket up and slightly right. FTR Jerry Messinger, 2003.

112 I Kings 6:7 ****5.11- or V1		The crux for this route is over as you pass the one bolt that protects the route. A **** rating is relative to the short boulder problem that it is. For that it's on eof the best in Southern Oregon. FA Mark Ivers and Jerry Harryman.

Linda New Comb and Fred.
Jerry Messinger

Route descriptions by Alfred Watson.

The Southern Oregon coast is known for its miles of spectacular beaches and breathtaking sunsets throughout the year. The next time you visit; don't forget to bring your climbing gear along for some memorable climbing next to the Pacific Ocean.
Rock formations on the coast, range from sea stack conglomerates, to sandstone, and marine basalt plugs. There is endless potential for bouldering on the south coast, but very few protected lines.

Caution: rock quality can be extremely variable especially on top of sea stacks.

Rogue

164 South Coast

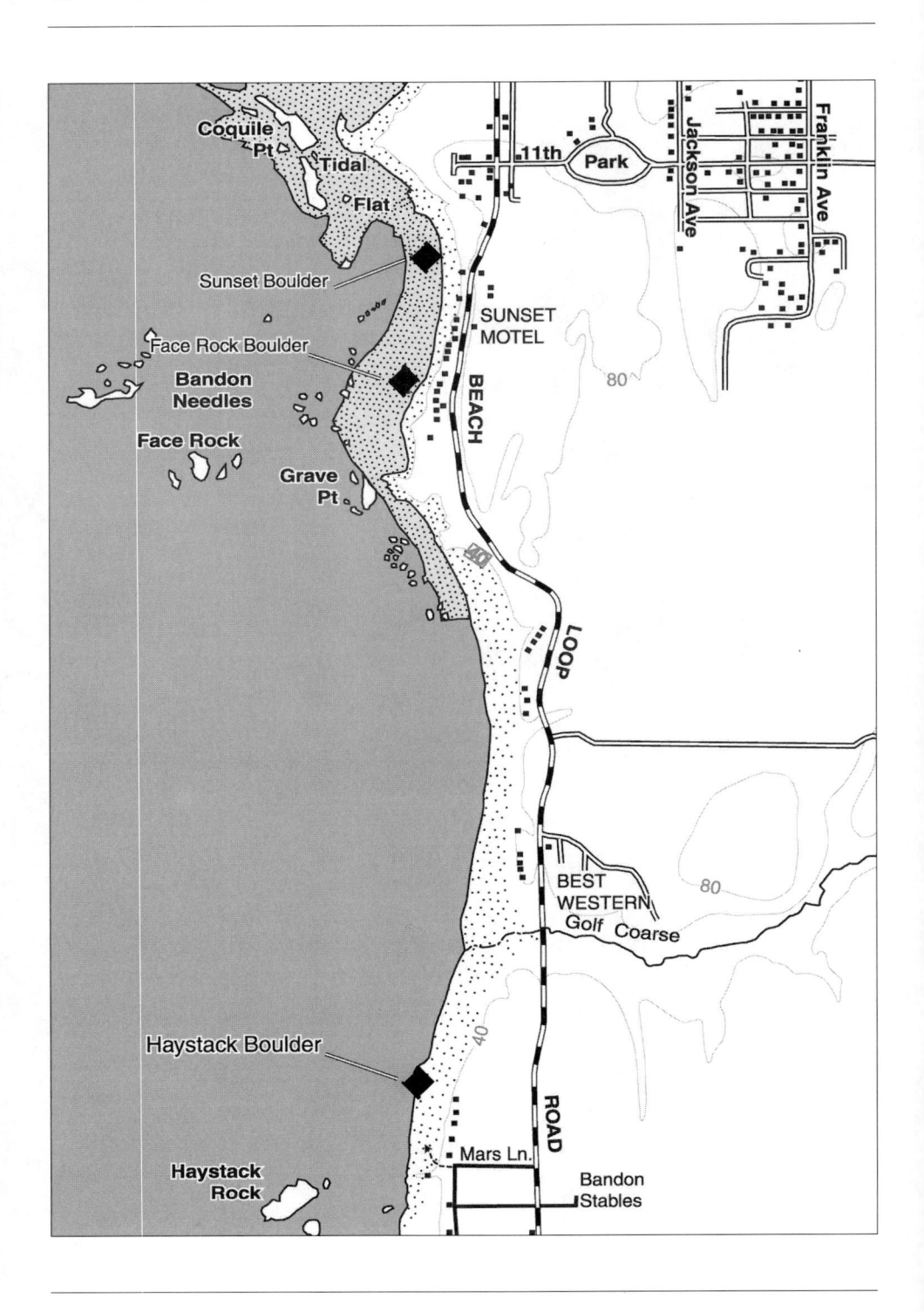

Coquile Pt
Tidal Flat
Sunset Boulder
Face Rock Boulder
Bandon Needles
Face Rock
Grave Pt
Haystack Boulder
Haystack Rock

11th Park
SUNSET MOTEL
BEACH LOOP
BEST WESTERN
Golf Coarse
Mars Ln.
Bandon Stables
ROAD

Jackson Ave
Franklin Ave

South Coast   165

BANDON
Once in old downtown Bandon. Head south along the coast to the Face Rock Scenic View Point.

SUNSET BOULDER
WGS84 10 T $^{03}83^{330m.}$E., $^{47}73^{587m.}$N.
This is a 40 foot blue schist boulder with exceptional rock quality throughout. Two sets of belay anchors can be found on top with several 1/2 inch holes for placing and removing 12mm Fixe Triplex bolts.

Access to the top of Sunset Boulder is by way a class 4 route on the northeast corner.

There are a large variety of climbing grades ranging from 5.5 shown here on the southeast corner to extreme climbing on the smooth overhanging west side of the Sunset Boulder.

Rogue

Eugene to Bandon	3 hours. Take OR-126 west to Florence and US-101 south to Bandon.
Roseburg to Bandon	2 hours. Take OR-99 west to Coquille. From Coquille travel soutwest to Bandon on OR-42S.
Medford to Bandon	3.5 hours. Take OR-99 west to Coquille. From Coquille travel soutwest to Bandon on OR-42S.

FACE ROCK BOULDER
WGS84 10 T $^{03}83^{333m.}$E., $^{47}71^{531m.}$N.
This is a 40 foot metavolcanic sea stack spire with marginal rock quality that is extremely variable. Several oxidized bolts and hangers are visible on the south face.

South face of the Face Rock Boulder with the approximate line shown. No information available. Caution: unknown quality top anchors.

Boulderer being spotted on the smooth west side of Sunset Boulder. Barbara Orton.

Rogue

HAYSTACK BOULDER

WGS84 10 T $^{03}83^{411m.}$E., $^{47}73^{936m.}$N.

This is a 40 foot blue schist sea stack spire with very good rock quality. Several oxidized bolts and hangers are visible northwest and west slab. A wide chimney on the eastside provides access to the top climbing to the south side of the large chockstone.

Haystack Boulder.

1 Chimney South Side **5.4

Approach the chimney that separates this rock from the south. Scramble about 15 feet up the short wall to the two bolts on top. Unprotected to top anchor.

2 Northwest Crack and Corner 5.6 (X) or TR

Scramble about 15 feet up the low angled northwest crack to a single bolt that is visible from the ground. From this point, climb right over the northwest corner onto the upper slab and better quality rock. Scramble up the slab to the two-bolt belay/TR anchors on top (5.1). Approximately 60 feet with one bolt.

3 Southwest Corner ***5.10a/b

Short and fun. Three bolts on the lower wall identify this route that climbs a short grippy steep 10 foot wall, mantle (.10a/b), and then friction right and up through polished schist (5.7) and onto the lower angled slab above, continuing to the bolted anchors on top (5.2). Approximately 60 feet with 3 bolts on the lower 20.

South Coast 169

Alfred Watson disappearing into the fog on Sun Kissed (5.8R), Kissing Rock.
Greg Orton

Rogue

170 South Coast

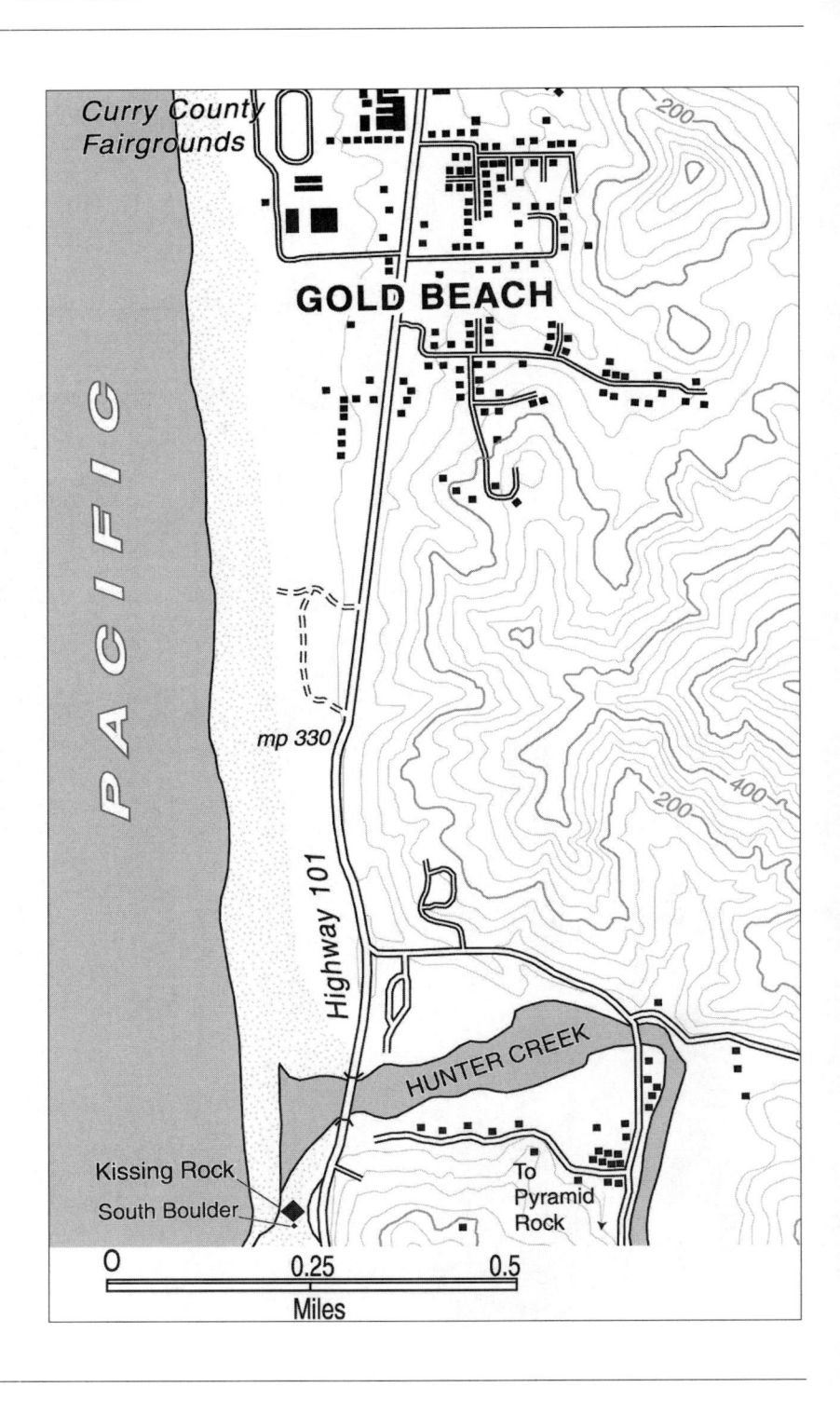

GOLD BEACH

Kissing Rock (approximately 200 feet high) is an ancient sea stack with a composition of volcanic breccia. This breccia is part of a mélange sequence which is composed of rocks that are scraped off the ocean floor and get stuck to the edge of the North American continental plate as the Pacific plate subducts under it.

Alfred Watson on First Kiss (5.11a), Kissing Rock. Greg Orton

Eugene to Gold Beach	4.5 hours. Take OR-126 west to Florence and US-101 south to Gold Beach.
Roseburg to Gold Beach	3.5 hours. Take OR-99 west to Coquille. From Coquille travel soutwest to Bandon on OR-42S.
Medford to Gold Beach	3.5 hours. Take US-99 southwest to Crescent City. From Crescent City travel north to Gold Beach on US-101.

KISSING ROCK

WGS84 10 T $^{03}82^{760m.}$E., $^{46}93^{661m.}$N.

Kissing Rock belongs to the Otter Point Formation. Kissing Rock is the first prominent rock just south of Gold Beach. From Gold Beach drive south on Highway 101 to milepost 337. Continue another 0.6 miles south, crossing Hunter Creek to Kissing Rock on your right. Park on the right in the large roadside pullout.

1 — First Kiss — **5.11a
This overhung climb is on the south side of Kissing Rock. The lower moves to the first bolt are bouldery and the distance to your first clip can vary from season to season depending on the level of the sand. Continue up 3 bolts on solid slightly overhanging jugs to the set of belay anchors. If the sand is high, this climb downgrades to 5.10+. Approx. 40 feet. FA Alfred Watson, 2000.

2 — Sun Kissed — ***5.8R
Starts 40 feet left of First Kiss. The first 40 feet is 4th class climbing to the first bolt. Follow the obvious ramp past a slightly off route 2nd bolt (bring a long sling for reduced drag) to a ledge. Proceed through the steeper crux past two more bolts to the summit of kissing rock! Approx. 200 feet, 5 bolts. FA Alfred Watson, 2001.

Right: South face of the South Boulder.
Opposite: West face Kissing Rock.
Alfred Watson.

3 Never Been Kissed ★★★5.6
This is a great lead for aspiring climbers. From *Sun Kissed* continue around to the northwest side of Kissing Rock where you'll find a large slab with a cave passing behind it. Before this slab was undermined by the sea and fell, it was possible for young couples to scramble to the top of Kissing Rock, thus earning it its name. This route climbs the slab's west arête to two bolted rappel/belay anchors. Approx. 40 feet, 2 bolts. FA Joelle and Alfred Watson, 2000.

4 French Kiss ★★★5.7 (TR)
Slab climb left of *Never Been Kissed*. Climb direct using the top anchors to *Never Been Kissed*. FA Joelle and Alfred Watson, 2000.

5 Kiss My Crack (South Boulder) ★★★5.9
This short south facing crack is just high enough to not let you forget to use those jams. This small rock is just below the parking area on the south-southeast corner of Kissing Rock. Approx. 35 feet high, gear up to 3 inches, walk off top. FA Joelle Watson, 2001.

MEYERS BEACH ROCK
WGS84 10 T $383^{778\text{-m.}}$E., $4683^{886\text{m.}}$N.
From Gold Beach drive south on Highway 101 to milepost 337 (Myers Creek Bridge). From milepost 337 continue another 0.6 miles south to the second long narrow pullout to your left just pass the Myers Creek Bridge. Meyers Beach Rock is one of several large igneous sea stacks on this beach. This particular rock is approximately 200 feet northwest of the parking area (Don't use a compass). The north side of the rock will have two cracks forming a "V" in the side of the rock. Four bolts have been placed on top for rappelling off, two at the top of Lil' Smokies and two on Ballpark.

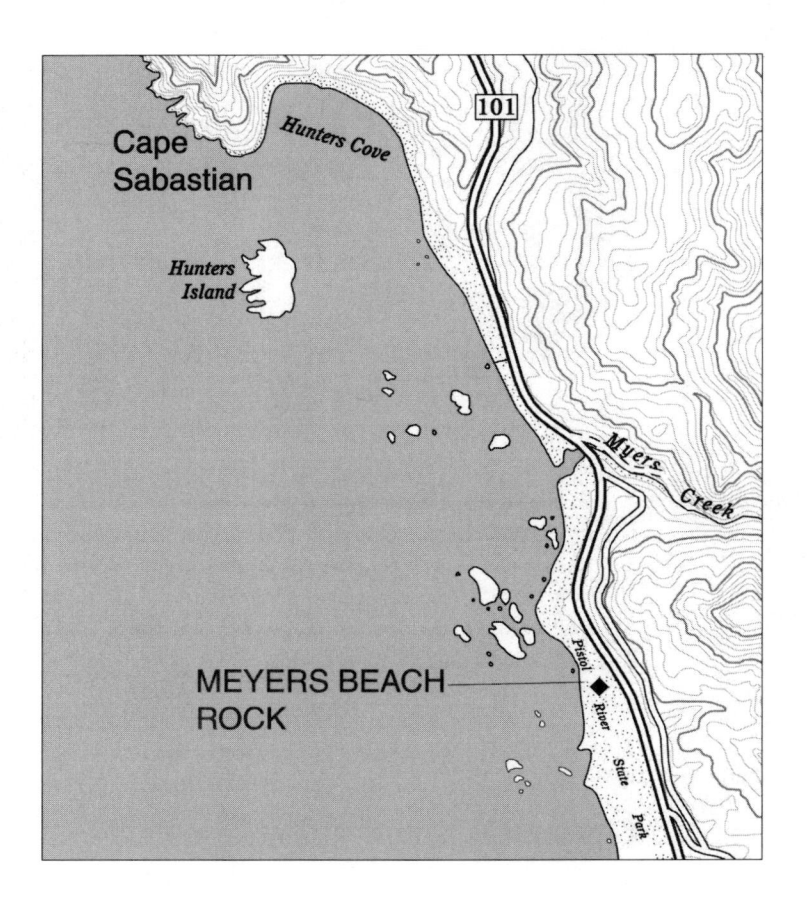

South Coast 175

Alfred Watson
First Kiss,
Kissing Rock.
Greg Orton

Rogue

176　South Coast

North Face
Meyers Rock

Alfred Watson

1
Oscar Meyers Left Crack
5.10a

This forgettable climb is 10 feet up from a shared start with the right crack. Follow the dirty, crumbly 1 to 2 inch left crack. This crack runs out 15 feet from the top with no opportunity for placements through this section. Rock quality also decreases near top. Approx 60 feet high. FA Alfred Watson, 2003.

2
Oscar Meyers Right Crack
***5.9**

This crack follows the right crack up the north side of rock. There are lots of opportunities for 1 to 4 inch placements. Rock quality decreases towards top. FA Alfred Watson, Steve DiCicco 2003.

3
Lil' Smokies
5.8R

You'll put your Lil' Smokies to work on this crack climb! The climb is on the ocean side of Meyers Creek rock. The start is 20 feet left of Ballpark. Scramble up 4th class section and ascend the arête using the dirty crack for pro. Crack runs out 15 feet before top. Anchors on top. Gear up to 2 inches. FA Alfred Watson, Steve DiCicco 2003.

4
Ballpark
***5.10c**

This face climb is on the Ocean side. TR only. Approx. 60 feet high. Anchors on top.

South Coast   177

West Face
Meyers Rock

Alfred Watson

Rogue

PYRAMID ROCK
WGS84 10 T ^{3}94$^{502m.}$E, ^{46}91$^{321m.}$N.

Elevation 2,818. Pyramid Rock is a metavolcanic marine basalt rock. It's polished West face is approximately 260 feet tall. Take the shorter East side trail from the parking area on Spur Road 195 to the summit where you will have a fantastic view of the coast range and find evidence of an old lookout.

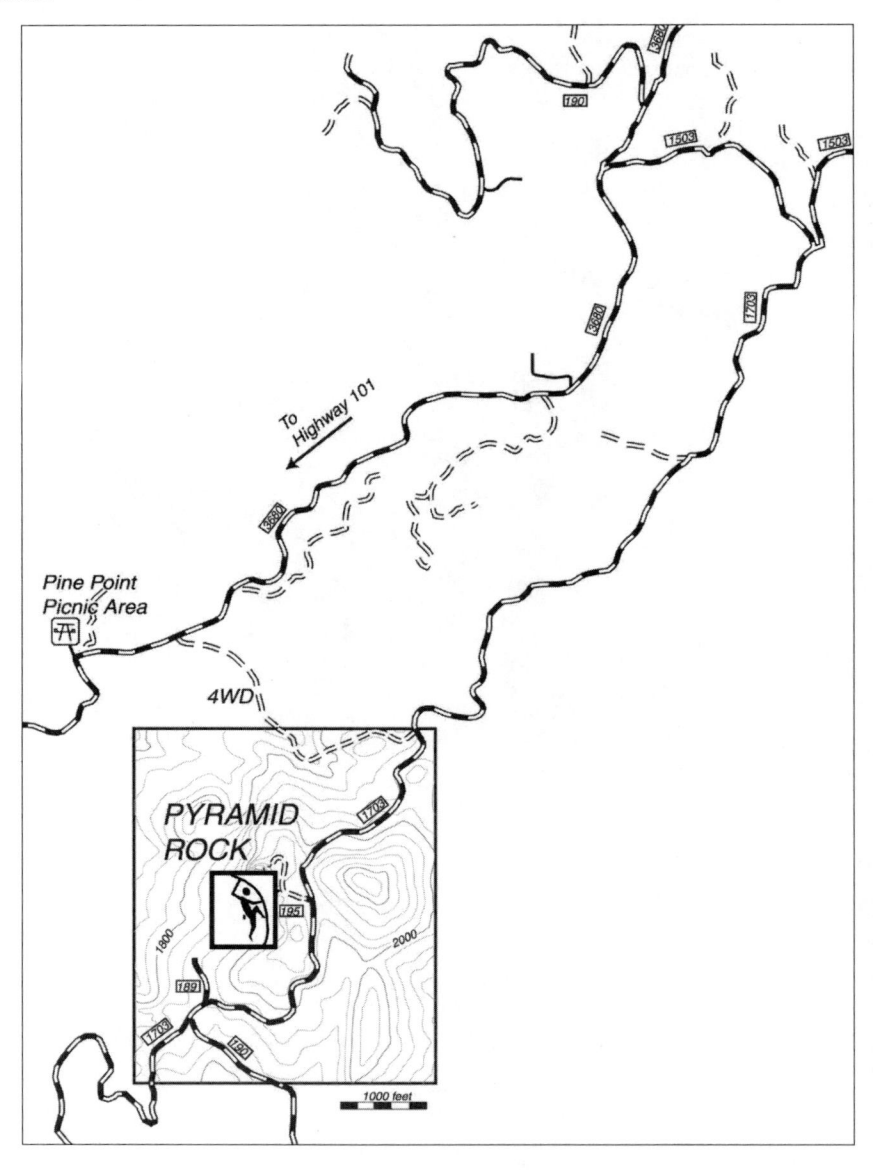

From Gold Beach take Highway 101 south 1.5 miles to Hunter Creek Road. This will be your first left south of Kissing Rock. Zero your Odometer.
From highway 101, turn left onto Hunter Creek road.
0.0 – 14.3 miles   Continue 14.3 miles on Hunter Creek Road (becoming FS Road-3680) turning right onto Forest Service Road 1503.
14.3 – 14.9 miles   Drive 0.6 miles up road 1503 turning right again onto Forest Service Road 1703.
14.9 – 17.2 miles   Drive 2.3 miles up road 1703, turning right onto Spur Road 195.
Park at the furthest convenient spot approximately 500 feet up the
road. (WGS84 10 T $^{03}94^{624}$, $^{46}91^{247}$). From the end of Spur
Road and at an old building foundation, follow the trail up the East
Ridge to the top of Pyramid Rock or contour the slope left around
to the steep south face ½ way up road.

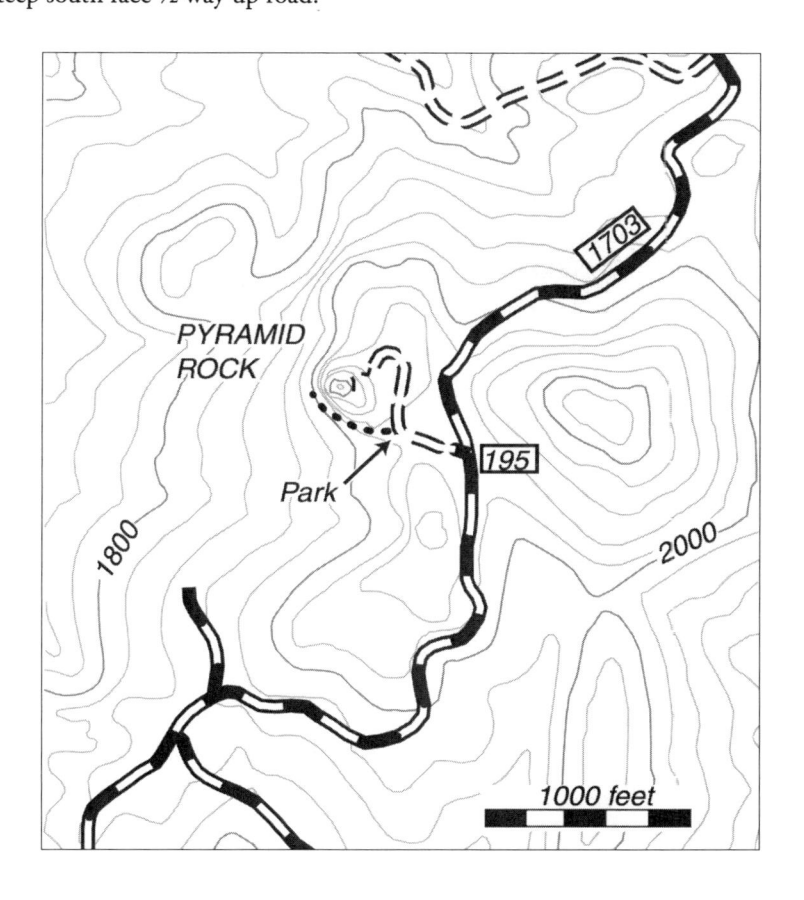

Rogue

South Coast

West Face
Pyramid Rock

1
Pacific Zone
5.11? Project

This overhanging, offwidth crack is on the West side of Pyramid Rock. Access to the bottom of the climb is ½ way up Spur Road 195 and then contours around the South side of the rock, scramble up the 4th class slab to reach the bottom of the crack. The obvious crack is visible from a long distance. Beware of sticker bushes in this crack. One bolt is at the top of this climb with opportunity for other passive anchors. Approximate height of the crack to the lower ledge is 190 feet.

JERRY MESSINGER

Jerry lives in Medford, Oregon with his wife Amy and children Issac (6), Levi (3), and Katie (1). He works as a Fire Warden with the State Department of Forestry.

Jerry has been climbing for 24 years. He remembers his first - first ascents as some unidentifiable lines in the Red Buttes Wilderness south of Applegate. He considers his most significant mentor to be Allan Watts, "He stood his ground during tumultuous times in the American climbing scene of the 80s and quietly redefined climbing in this country by his spirit for pushing the limits, if not on his accomplishments alone."

Memorable ascent: Joshua Tree, 1987. "Ripping my fingers of a 5.8+ and falling 35 feet. A local later told me the + was the .11c move on the othewise 5.8 route!"

JOE CHAVES

Joe lives outside of Ashland, Oregon where he has a private Forest Managment Company.

Joe has been climbing for 18 years.
He lists Jerry Messinger as becoming a significant mentor to his climbing.

Favorite quote: "Heeh, heeh-heeh, heeh."— *Beavis*
Most Memorable ascent: *Salathe*, Yosemite.

Recommended southwest Oregon routes: *The Prize* (.11c) on Old Man Rock (Umpqua); *New Year's Day* (.10c) on Rattlesnake; *Six-Cheetahs* (.10c), on Greensprings; *The Metro* (.11a) on Rattlesnake; *Roundabout* (.10d) on Pilot Rock; *and Sniff* (.11d), Emigrant Lake.

ALFRED WATSON

Alfred lives in Gold Beach, Oregon with Joelle and the twins Molly and Brooke (Born August 2004). He works as a Civil Engineer with the United States Forest Service.

Alfred began rock climbing at Greensprings as a self-taught 18-year old. He remembers his first lead was Hairway to Steavan. Joelle and Alfred, both avid climbers, were engaged on pitch-3 of Super Slab at Smith Rock. "Luckily she decided to wear the ring for the rappel down because I dropped the ring's box."

When I asked what his most memorable experience climbing has been he stated without hesitation, "being on the road with Joelle, all the incredible places we have visited, experiences that we have had, and people that we have met along the way."

Favorite quote: "Not everything that counts can be counted; and not everthing that can be counted counts." — *Albert Einstein*

Recommended southwest Oregon routes: Sky Patrol (.10a) on Greensprings; Sunkist (.8) on Kissing Rock; and Scary Turtles (.11) in the Callahans.

GREG ORTON

Greg lives in Roseburg, Oregon with Barbara (Bobbie) and their son Chandler. He works as a Soil Scientist for the Umpqua National Forest. The Orton family work together along with climbing partner Harold Hall instructing climbing classes for Umpua Community College.

Greg has 25 years of climbing experience and has been actively climbing in western Oregon for the past 15 years. He says he began climbing in the Eastern Sierra, however his mother tells a story of a panicked neighbor coming over one morning because a 2-year old was sitting on top the roof. His mother decided the safest thing at that point was to teach Greg to down-climb.

Greg considers his mentors to have been Robert Stavely (SP) Parker, Doug Robinson, and Harold Hall. He considers his favorite western Oregon climbs to be The Peregrine Traverse (.7), HangTen (.10a), The Newt (.10c), and Black Magic (.10d).

Favorite encouragements: "If you don't fall your not climbing to your full potential." and "There's a great foothold by your right ear."

The Rogue Index

Ashland Boulders	49 – 63
Mtn. Ashland	65 – 68
Emigrant Lake	69 – 84
Greensprings	85 – 96
Pilot Rock	97 – 104
Rabbit Ears	105 – 119
Rattlesnake	121 – 162
Bandon	163 – 168
Gold Beach	170 – 180

V0-
Look Ma No Hands	128

V0
The Fall of Booger	61
Got Wood	56
Leap year	54
Scratch	58
Staircas	56
Trail Boulder Slab	52
Unnamed, Crack	58
Unnamed, Nifty	56
Unnamed, Slappy	61
Unnamed, Slappy	63
Waco	57

V0+
Alcove	54
Deception	53
Freudian Slip	52
Mr. Chainsaw	61
I Peter 2:7 & 8 ***	161
Poison	53
Slabby Galore	61
Slappy Gilmore	63
Static	54
Undercling Problem	58
Unnamed, Slappy	61
Unnamed, Slappy	62
Unnamed, Slappy	63
World's Sexiest Offwidth	59

V1
Ashen Ghoul	56
Bloodbath	59
Bottom Feeder	53
Contrive This	63
Death Mantle	60
Disco Superfly	58
Double Mantle	59
Fornication	56
I Kings 6:7 ****	162
I Psalm 89:26	162
Seamin'	60
Shoot the Messinger	57
Traverse	61
Unnamed, Disco	58
Unnamed, Split	59
Unnamed, ZZtop	54
Wailing Soul	54
Wax	63

V2
Basic	59
Crack of Doom	56
Crack for the Masses	53
Flakes	54
Gammy's Gettin' Upset	60
Intro Crack	52
Just Less Dope	60
Karma Police	129
Limber	57
Low Start	52

Rogue

Index

REM	54
A Special Place in Hell…	59
Telekenesis	58
Tiny Dancer	53
Unnamed, Acid Castle	61
Unnamed, Doom	56
Unnamed, Hidden	53
Unnamed, Slappy	63
Unnamed, ZZTop52	
Wake Up the Monkey	59
The Way We Were	58
ZZTop	55

V3

Castle in the Sky	61
Crimpslap	58
Joe's Problem	55
The Laying On of Hands	8
Unnamed (var), Split	59

<5.7

Amp Chimney	67
Mr. Anderson	73
Axe Wound ***	96
The Bowl	115
Chimney	94
East Ear Summit	108
Fire!	73
Graffiti Rock	67
Haystack NW Crack	168
Hippie Teacher	73
Lucky Rabbit's Foot	113
Marge Simpson's Bac.	87
Never Been Kissed ***	174
Pilots License	103
Science Barbie	156
Snowblind	67
Sunset Boulder ***	165
Tool Shed	73
West Chimney	108
West Ear Summit	108

5.7

Alien Life Forms	88
Beavis	75
Dihedral	67
Domes Do It	113
First Blood ***	91
French Kiss ***	173
Graffiti Rock	67
Nachos	77
Poison Oak Crack	84
Polish Photo Route	109
Procrastinating Aliens	88
Snake-N-Flake	91
Tricks for the Kids ***	113
White Slab Crack	67
Wimpy ****	77

5.8

Board Head ***	67
Bowling for Bunnies	113
Bug Off ***	75
Burritos***	77
Butthead	75
Chain Links var.	90
The Clam	160
Crash Landing ***	101
Graffiti Rock	67
Janeivour	146
Lil' Smokies	160
Marge's Naval	87
Off-width ***	92
Pet Semitary	80
Pocket Change	85
Positive 4 Street	116
Procrastinating Aliens	88
Razor Crack ***	95
Shasta	129
Southwest Arete	100
Sun Kissed ***	172

The Rogue Index

5.9

Barney	137
Blitzfart	93
Deep Purple	90
Graffiti Rock	67
Kiss My Crack ***	173
Late Again ***	67
Mountain Jam	93
Oscar Meyer's Right Crack	176
Paul's Crack	94
Skimpy Var.	79
Slippery When Wet	113
Tango n' Torture	115
Uppyer Crack	127

5.10a

Annita Hill Mem…	67
Aqua Weenie	84
Arabesque ****	141
Arete ***	116
Beyond the Siskiyou Sky	80
Boomer	129
Bus Ride	77
Chinese Water Torture	150
Cornholio ***	75
Dark Shadows	153
Dihedral/Arete to Face	67
Footloose	115
Gavin's Straight Up ***	112
Gray Matter	160
Long Dong Silver	67
Mountain Lion's Perch	139
Oscar Meyer's Left Crack	178
Rain Dance ****	118
Rain Sucks	149
Sky Patrol ****	88
Slippery Gold ****	115
Sound Tracker	130
Spaghetti Var.	77
Split Decision ***	143
Velcro	118

5.10a/b

Blockade	159
Haystack SW Corner ***	168
Isaiah 2:21	162
Ski Tracks	90

5.10b

Aqua Man ****	84
The Bolted Barbie	156
Butt Bar Express	130
Fishhooks on the Whip	67
Fluff's Route	142
Carson Hall	156
Opie & Andie ***	69
Ren	78
Step Up ***	103
White Slab Left ***	67

5.10b/c

Jonser	91
Ringer	146

5.10c

2 North	154
Arching Crack ***	116
Ballpark	176
Chain Links	90
Child's Play ****	110
Chowder	160
Flight of the Dead Souls ****	153
Knobland	91
Six Cheetas ****	87
Test Tube	94
Thumper ***	126

5.10c/d

Birthday Bash	138
Hairway to Steavan ****~	88
In Oregon We Rust ***	149
I Peter 2:7 & 8 ***	161
New Years Day ***	138

Index

5.10d
Bird of Prey	139
Black Swan	152
East Berlin	158
The Great Bear	130
Indigo	141
Inflatable Man	96
Keep the Fat ***	92
Misty Horizon	149
Ocelot	127
Other Kid	75
Panic	116
Roundabout ****	101
Skimpy ***	79
Sportholio ***	115
Strange Force ****	112
Thin Crack	94
White Slab Right	67

5.10d/.11a
Aurora ***	126
I Kings 6:7 ****	162
I Psalm 89:26	162
Rain Man ***	149
West Berlin	159

5.11a
Airlift	159
Beavis Buddies	137
Broken Brain ***	124
Buttmunch	73
Cloudburst	149
The Dagger ***	132
Euphoria ***	96
First Kiss	172
Frozen ***	148
Full Marge ***	87
Gavin's Straight Up ***	112
Horizon Air	149
Ice Man ***	134
KaraKorum ***	153
Little Lucy ***	125
Magic Blocks ****	102
Master Hwang	156
The Metro ****	158
Mexican Summer ***	93
Razor Crack var. ****	95
Rock Dancer	139
Secret Window	140
Schizophrenia	132
Shag-Eared Villain	116
Sunset Arete ***	161
TR variations	80
Woman in the Mist	133

5.11a/b
Hard Man	84
Kooch Master ***	94
Secret Forest	139
Stimpy ****	78
Yosemite Crack	94

5.11b
Boys Who Ain't French ***	88
Chainsaw Psycho Dork ****	156
Free Goo	94
Lady in Red ***	143
The Shadow	142
Sunny Delight	133
Topaz	133

5.11c
Back Bonker Arete ***	73
Bat Flight Express	146
Capt. Horatio Horn Blower ***	83
Cloud Drifter	131
Comfortably Numb ***	154
Gloo ***	80
Green M&M's	67
Green Screams ****	90
Loose Ends ****	88
Mirror Image	143
Shadowlands ***	92
Whistler ***	132

Western Oregon

The Rogue Index

5.11c/d
Lost Horizon	148

5.11d
Angela	139
Ikenseaor Crack ***	140
Pain	115
Shadow Caster ****	143
Sniff ****	83

5.11d/.12a
Borealis ***	126

5.12a
Captain Quaalude ***	156
Charybdis ***	144
Devastator ***	80
Full Circle ****	136
The Groove ***	140
Rufous	133
Scorpion ****	153
TR variations	80

5.12a/b
Little Fatty	134
Not Forgotten	143
Rattlesnake Reality ****	136
Red Sky	161
TR Problem	161

5.12b
Afterburner ***	148
Girl with Flaxen Hair ****	135
Leisure Days ***	139
Reefer Finish	80
Welcome to Oregon ***	149

5.12b/c
Galoshes	150
Pleasure Victim ****	158
Psychadelicatessen ****	137

5.12c
Full Link Up ****	80

5.13a
Amy ****	39

Aid
Jolt (Ac, 5.12d)	131
Orange Crush (Ac, 5.12b)	130
Red Bull (Ac, 5.12b/c)	130

A	Asay, Don	89, 95, 96
	Asay, John	xix, 76
	Asay, Nick	96
B	Benham, Randy	xx, 115
	Bagshaw, Sean	73
	Bucey, Mandy	xiii, 77
C	Chaves, Joe	xx, xxi, xxii, 81, 85, 87, 92, 94, 97, 101, 102, 104, 105, 109, 110, 112, 114, 115, 116, 126, 127, 130, 132, 133, 136, 137, 139, 146, 149, 154, 156, 158
	Coddington, Emma	156
	Crews, Steve	115
D	Davis, Jim	xx, xxii, 65, 69, 75, 77, 78, 80, 84, 121, 129, 75
	DiCicco, Steve	176
	Dodge, Nicholas A.	xvi, xviii, 97, 105
	Dowling, Bob	113
	Drake, Jessica	89
E	Eggleston, Andy	120
	Ekstrand, Bob	xviii
	Elder, Chris	xxii, 85
F	Ferguson, Gavin	xx, 87, 94, 112
H	Hall, Harold	xxxvi
	Heismith, Sam	114
	Higgins, Dan	xx, 80, 83, 84, 67, 94, 96
I	Iverse, Mark	115, 162
J	Johnson, Steve	75
	Jones, Cory	xx, 88, 90, 91, 132, 133, 134, 135, 140, 155
K	Kerr, Nathan	80
	Kerr-Velentic, Mahlon	xxii, 85
	Knapp, Brandon	xxv
L	Layton, M	xviii, 105, 108
	Lee, Michael	xx, 113

NAMES

M	Messinger, Jerry	xv, xvii, xx, xxii, 69, 75, 77, 78, 79, 80, 81, 83, 65, 85, 105, 120, 121, 126, 127, 129, 131, 132, 133, 134, 135, 136, 137, 138, 139, 140, 143, 144, 145, 146, 147, 148, 149, 150, 151, 152, 153, 154, 155, 156, 157, 158, 159, 160, 161, 162
	Morell, Josh	111, 119
N	NewComb, Bill	xx, xxii, xxiii, 87, 126, 130, 133, 139, 141, 142, 143, 146, 152, 153
	NewComb, Linda	62
O	Orton, Barbara	167
	Orton, Greg	xvii, xix, xxi, xxiii, xv, xxxvii, 64, 73, 76, 77, 101, 104, 147, 151, 169, 175
P	Porter, Chuck	xx, xxi, xxii, 97, 101, 102, 103, 112
R	Ransom, Don	xx, xxii, 88, 105, 113, 115, 116, 118
	Ransom, Dylan	xxii, 49, 116, 118
	Rasmussen, Darryl	111, 113
	Rodriguez, John	95
S	Schlep, Wendy	145
	Schmidt, Scott	xviii,
	Scott, Jim	xviii,
	Shannan, Jim	73
	Smallwood, Jim	xx, 88, 96
	Sohl, Chris	115
U	Uhtoff, Pat	101
W	Watson, Alfred	163, 169, 173, 175, 176, 177
	Watson, Joelle	xxi, 173
	Weiseth, Matt	115
	White, W.	xviii, 105, 108

Notes and topos

Names

Notes and topos

ACCESS: IT'S EVERYONE'S CONCERN

The Access Fund is a national nonprofit climbers' organization working to keep climbing areas open and conserve the climbing environment. Please consider these principles when climbing.

- **ASPIRE TO CLIMB WITHOUT LEAVING A TRACE:** Pick up litter and leave trees and plants intact.
- **MAINTAIN A LOW PROFILE:** Minimize noise and yelling at the crag.
- **DISPOSE OF HUMAN WASTE PROPERLY:** Use toilets whenever possible. If toilets are not available, dig a "cat hole" at least six inches deep and 200 feet from any water, trails, campsites or the base of climbs. Always pack out toilet paper.
- **USE EXISTING TRAILS:** Cutting switchbacks causes erosion.
- **BE DISCRETE WITH FIXED ANCHORS:** Avoid placing bolts unless they are absolutely necessary.
- **RESPECT THE RULES:** Speak up when other climbers do not. Expect restrictions in designated wilderness areas, rock art sites and caves. Power drills are illegal in wilderness and all national parks.
- **PARK AND CAMP IN DESIGNATED AREAS:** Some climbing areas require a permit for overnight camping.
- **RESPECT PRIVATE PROPERTY:** Be courteous to landowners.
- **JOIN THE ACCESS FUND:** To become a member, make a tax-deductible donation of $35.

P.O. Box 17010
Boulder, CO 80308
303-545-6772
www.accessfund.org

ACCESS FUND
your climbing future